IMPRIMI POTEST
Kanzenze, 12-2-1952
P. SIMEON, o.f.m.
Sup. Reg.

IMPRIMATUR
Luabo-Kamina, 30-5-1952
† VICTOR PETRUS KEUPPENS
Vic. Ap. de Lulua

BANTU PHILOSOPHY

by

The Revd. Father PLACIDE TEMPELS

(Translated into English from « La Philosophie Bantoue »,
the French Version by Dr A. Rubbens of Fr. Tempels' original
work. The Revd. Colin King, M.A. Translator,)

With a Foreword to the English Edition by Dr Margaret
Read, C.B.E., Ph. D., M,A., formerly Professor of Education
and Head of the Departement of Education in Tropical Areas,
The University of London, Institute of Education.

IMPRIMATUR

† Victor Petrus Keuppens
Vic. Ap. de Lulua
Luauo-Kamina, 30-5-1952

CONTENTS

CHAPTER I

IN SEARCH OF A BANTU PHILOSOPHY

CHAPTER II

BANTU ONTOLOGY

CHAPTER III

BANTU WISDOM OR CRITERIOLOGY

FOREWORD
to the English Translation

The Rev. Colin King has, in this translation of
Father Tempels' study of Bantu philosophy, con-
ferred a great benefit on those students of African life
and thought who use the English language for reading. Ever since I saw the French edition published by
Lovania in 1945, I have recommended the study to
all who could use it in French. I have memories, too,
of more than one African or Sudanese or Chinese
student, who did not read French, sitting beside an
English fellow student in the little seminar room
under the roof, while they worked together on the
ideas put forward by Father Tempels with such intimate knowledge and eloquence. Every year, in the
seminar to which Mr. King refers, someone raises a
question touching on the philosophic thought of African peoples. When they are referred to Father Tempels' study, there has often been dismay because it
has only been available in French. Mr. King himself,
as he says in his Translator's Note, worked on an

English translation for his own continuous use and very generously made it available for use by others in the Department in which he holds at present a post as lecturer.

It was clear, however, that for the English-speaking world here was a great need to have access to this study, and all of us who have made use of it in the past will welcome the fact that an English edition is now available.

MARGARET READ
Professor of Education.
Head of the Department of Education
in Tropical Areas,
University of London, Institue of Education.

August, 1953.

NOTE
by the English Translator

"La Philosophie Bantoue" was first published by Lovania at Elizabethville, in the Belgian Congo, in 1945, and was a French translation made by Dr. A. Rubbens. Copies of this version of the work became very difficult to obtain because those who had been able to snap them up in the short time during which they were available were mostly scholars who constantly needed their copies for their own use or for the use of their pupils. To some extent this situation was relieved by the publication by De Sikkel in Antwerp of the original Dutch text and of a revised French translation, also by Dr. A. Rubbens, in the Collection Présence Africaine in Paris.

It was my original intention merely to make a private translation for my own edification and for consultation by students in the Colonial Department (now the Department of Education in Tropical Areas) of the Institute of Education at London University, where my introduction to the work in

Dr. Margaret Read's Advanced Seminar for the Study of Society was one of many invaluable benefits thence derived. At that time I had access to the first French translation only.

When I had got so far, it was impressed upon me that a published English translation was widely and urgently needed. I was able to secure copies of the original Dutch and of the revised French versions ; and when the Revd. Father Tempels very kindly accepted my offer of my English translation, he gave me invaluable guidance in the necessary revision. The present translation has taken cognizance of the original Dutch ant the revised French versions ; and it also incorporates many details supplied by Fr. Tempels and now appearing for the first time. While thus most gratefully acknowledging all that Fr. Tempels has put into this translation. I must also pay tribute to a great deal of help with the Dutch text from Mr. J.L. Preforius who is both a Dutch scholar (which I am not) and also an experienced educational missionary among the Bantu. He was able to explain to me many matters of Bantu usage upon which I was ignorant or doubtful.

There are inevitable difficulties in translating Bantu philosophy into European terminology, and Fr. Tempels' own Dutch original is itself necessarily in part a translation. The problem is referred to by Fr. Tempels himself in Chapter II (p. 26).

There are often linguistic problems of terminology. One concerns the selection of the word to be used to translate the French "la force" and "force vitale",

used to denote the Bantu basic concept of the ultimate nature of being, as we should call it. The Dutch
version uses two words, "kracht" and "sterkte", both
alone and in combination with "levens", but both are
rendered by the French "force".

Another relates to many references to Africans in
the book. My general rule has been to speak of
"Africans" whenever I could not with assured accu-
racy speak of "Bantu". On p. 146, where I had no
option but to use "Black Race", I italicised it. I
dislike the terms "native(s)", "primitive...", and, still
more, "savages". The last is employed (in italics)
only in a context which shows that Fr. Tempels'
dislike of the term is as great as my own. For the
rest, I hardly imagine that any reader of this translation will think that either Fr. Tempels or I entertain
the least derogatory thought in respect of people (or
peoples) not of the "White race". It is my hope that
this translation will assist many to find, in the stimu-
lating thought of Fr. Tempels' work, a key to a fuller
understanding of African peoples and a deeper grasp
of the truth that the true philosophy is that which
both accepts and rejects all philosophies ; but, in
regard to peoples, rejects none : accepting all as they
are and as they will become.

PREFACE

My excellent friend, the Ȓevd. Father Placide Tempels, has asked me for a short preface. I cannot do better than to reproduce the following passage from a letter which I received from him when I had just ended my short colonial career.

"It is a curious fact that it was many challenging statements and casts of thought in your "Elements of Negro Customary Law" that obliged me to *concretize* and *synthetize* my own thought.

"I felt baffled, not because the Elements which you treat are false, but because, raising so profoundly the real question at issue and examining it, they wander round the point a little until the last moment and do not drive the nail right home.

"When you wrote to me "What then do you regard as the African way of synthesizing ideas ?" you were feeling the lacuna or imperfection in your own conceptions, your own discoveries. Without this lacuna I should certainly never have sought to develop this synthesis as I have."

"Tribal law, primitive philosophy and an applied catechism will become, I believe, a trio of insepar-ables."

Already, he wrote to me, certain Missionaries were using with the greatest success principles of life drawn from Bantu ways of thinking.

It would be false modesty on our part not to see that ethnology, ethnological principles, ethnological jurisprudence and the religious instruction of patriar-chal peoples will derive a new and a fresh orientation by reason of the Revd. Fr. Tempels' work.

Up to the present, ethnographers have denied all abstract thought to tribal peoples. The civilized Christian European was exalted, the savage and pagan primitive man was denigrated. Out of this concept a theory of colonisation was born which now threatens to fail everywhere.

A true estimate of indigenous peoples can now take the place of the misunderstanding and fanati-cism of the ethnology of the past and of the former attitude of aversion entertained with regard to them.

That is why this present work by the Revd. Fr. Tempels is destined to achieve so much good. It will mark a new epoch in the history of colonisation. Europe will only enhance its prestige by admitting, in the light of Fr. Tempels' thought, its former ethnolog-ical mistakes.

Since the Greeks, all classical European philosophy

has revealed a static outlook. But older peoples, tribal peoples as I call them — since, whether they are patrilineal or matrilineal, they are all patriarchal — have preserved a mental outlook not purely static. We have behind us two thousand years of too static thought. Prof. Maréchal, some years ago, ended his study of Kant as follows : "The future metaphysics will be either dynamic or it will not be at all."

We await a neo-Thomism, with Mercier, Maritain and many others who are seeking a modern Thomism. Without a system of thought, philosophical and personal, attaining that exactly, no objectivity in ethnography is possible.

It is precisely from this standpoint that the Rev. Fr. Tempels' work throws such remarkable light on ethnography today and will so remarkably illumine colonial practice and missionary evangelization tomorrow.

We are in with him on the ground floor of modern thought.

Brussels, 20th July, 1945.

E. Possoz.

CHAPTER I

IN SEARCH OF A BANTU PHILOSOPHY

1. *Life and death determine human behaviour.*

It has been often remarked that an European who has given up, during his life, all practice of the Christian religion, quickly returns to a Christian viewpoint when suffering or pain raise the problem of the preservation and survival or the loss and destruction of his being. Many sceptics turn, in their last moments, to seek in the ancient Christian teaching of the West, the *practical answer* to the problem of redemption or destruction. Suffering and death are ever the two great apostles who lead many wanderers in Europe at their last moments to our traditional Christian wisdom.

In the same way among our Bantu we see the *évolués* [1], the "civilized", even the Christians, return to their former ways of behaviour whenever they

---

1. *Évolués* : I preserve this term untranslated for lack of a suitable English equivalent. It signifies those who have passed out of the traditional ways of life and thought of their own ethnic group and have taken over those of the West. (C.K.)

are overtaken by moral lassitude, danger or suffering. They do so because their ancestors left them *their practical solution* of the great problem of humanity, the problem of life and death, of salvation or destruction. The Bantu, only converted or civilized superficially, return at the instance of a determining force to the behaviour atavistically dictated to them.

Among the Bantu and, indeed, among all primitive peoples, life and death are the great apostles of fidelity to a magical view of life and of recourse to traditional magical practices.

2. *All human behaviour depends upon a system of principles.*

If the modern over-civilized European is unable to be entirely emancipated from the attitudes of his ancestors, it is because his reactions are founded upon a complete philosophical system, influenced by Christianity ; upon a clear, complete, positive intellectual conception of the universe, of man, of life and death, and of the survival of a spiritual principle called the soul. This view of the visible and invisible world is too deeply ingrained in the spirit of Western culture not to rise up again irresistibly when the great crises of life occur.

It is very possible, both with the individual and with the tribal or culture group, that the mysteries of life and death, survival and destruction, together with fear arising from all these mysteries, became the psychological agent that gave birth to certain behaviour patterns and to certain redemptive practices. It would, however, scarcely be scientific to retain, as the sole ground of human behaviour, the influence of environment and of psychological factors (emotion, fantasy, or childish imagination). We do not study the attitudes of a few individuals. We compare two conceptions of life—the Christian on the one hand and the magical on the other—which have perpetuated themselves through time and in space : two conceptions which, in the course of centuries, whole peoples and entire cultures have embraced.

The persistence of these attitudes through centuries of simultaneous evolution can only be satisfactorily explained by the presence of a corpus of logically co-ordinated intellectual concepts, a "Lore". Behaviour can be neither universal nor permanent unless it is based upon a concatenation of ideas, a logical system of thought, a complete positive philosophy of the universe, of man and of the things which surround him, of existence, life, death and of the life beyond.

Without excluding other factors (divine and human) we must postulate, seek and discover a logical system of human thought as the ultimate foundation of any logical and universal system of human behaviour.

No live code of behaviour is possible unless the meaning of life is sensed. There can be no will to determine life unless the ends of life are conceived.

No one can pursue the way to redemption who has no philosophy of salvation.

In the matter of the religion of primitive peoples, modern science seems to have concluded quite definitely, by the light of the methods of historical criticism, that present beliefs of primitive and semi-primitive peoples had their origin in simple notions which have degenerated today into complex conceptions ; and in precise, exact principles that have evolved towards imprecision and inexactness. It is today generally admitted that, among primitive peoples, it is the most primitive of all who have maintained the most pure form of the concept of the Supreme Being, Creator and Disposer of the Universe.

The faith of really primitive peoples in the Supreme Being lies at the root of all the religious conceptions current among semi-primitives : animism, dynamism, fetichism and magic.

Need we, then, be astonished that we find among the Bantu, and more generally among all primitive peoples, as the foundation upon which their intellectual conception of the universe rests, certain basic principles and even a system of philosophy—though it is relatively simple and primitive—derived from a logically coherent ontology ?

Many roads seem to lead to the discovery of such an ontological system. A profound knowledge of the language, a penetrating study of their ethnology, a critical investigation of their laws, or again, the adaptation of religious teaching to primitive thinking : all these can reveal it to us.

It is also possible—and this is obviously the shortest way—to trace directly the thought of the Bantu on the deepest matters, to penetrate it and to analyse it. Has Bantu philosophy been studied and developed as such ? If not, it is high time that each scholar should start to seek out and define the fundamental thought underlying Bantu ontology, the one and only key that allows native thought to be penetrated.

We need not expect the first African who comes along, especially the young ones, to be able to give us a systematic exposition of his ontological system. None the less, this ontology exists ; and it penetrates and informs all the thought of these primitives ; it dominates and orientates all their behaviour.

It is our task to trace out the elements of this thought, to classify them and to systematise them according to the ordered systems and intellectual disciplines of the Western world.

Anyone who claims that primitive peoples possess no system of thought, excludes them thereby from the category of men. Those who do so, contradict themselves fatally elsewhere. To give one example only, we find it in R. Allier, who, in his "Psychology of Conversion" writes, (p. 138) "If you ask the Ba-Souto, says Mr. Dieterlen, the why and the wherefore of these customs, they cannot tell you. They do not indulge in reflective thought. They have no theories and no doctrines. The only thing that matters, they think, is the carrying out of certain traditional acts, preserving contact with the past and with the dead." But two pages further on we read, "What is it which

causes this opposition of the chiefs to be irresistible ?
It is the fear of breaking the mystic bond which,
through the chiefs, is established with the ancestors
and the fear of the disasters which that may entail."
What is this "mystic bond" or what is this "ancestral
influence" if not the elements of a system of
thought ? Is it a simple instinct or an irrational fear
and no more ? Would it not be more reasonable and
more scientific to look for whatever *ideas* sustain this
reaction to the "mystic bond" ? Perhaps, after that,
we may be able to do without the omnibus word
"mystic".

3. *The reasons for seeking the intellectual instrument, the fundamental philosophical concepts and
   principles of the Bantu* [1].

Any one who wishes to study primitive people or
évolués must give up all idea of attaining valid scientific conclusions so long as he has not been able to
understand their metaphysic. To declare on *a priori*
grounds that primitive peoples have no ideas on the
nature of beings, that they have no ontology and that
they are completely lacking in logic, is simply to turn
one's back on reality. Every day we are able to note

---

1. See my Translator's Foreword on the use of the names
"African" and "Bantu " passim. (C.K.)

that primitive peoples are by no means just children afflicted with a bizarre imagination. It is as Men that we have learned to know them in their homes. Folk-lore alone and superficial descriptions of strange customs cannot enable us to discover and understand primitive man. Ethnology, linguistics, psycho-analysis, jurisprudence, sociology and the study of religions are able to yield definitive results only after the philosophy and the ontology of a primitive people have been thoroughly studied and written up. If, in fact, primitive peoples have a concrete conception of being and of the universe, this "ontology" of theirs will give a special character, a local colour, to their beliefs and religious practices, to their mores, to their language, to their institutions and customs, to their psychological reactions and, more generally, to their whole behaviour. It is even more true, I venture to think, that the Bantu, like primitive people in general, live more than we do by Ideas and by following their own ideas.

So much must be said for the benefit of those who wish to "study" the Bantu and primitive peoples generally.

Nevertheless, a better understanding of the realm of Bantu thought is just as indispensable for all who are called upon to live among native people. It therefore concerns all colonials, especially those whose duty is to hold administrative or judicial office among African people; all those who are concerning themselves with a felicitous development of tribal law; in short, it concerns all who wish to civilize,

educate and raise the Bantu. But, if it concerns all
colonizers with good will, it concerns most particularly missionaries.

If one has not penetrated into the depths of the
personality as such, if one does not know on what
basis their acts come about, it is not possible to
understand the Bantu. One is entering into no spiritual contact with them. One cannot make oneself
intelligible to them, especially in dealing with the
great spiritual realities. On the contrary, one runs the
risk, while believing that one is "civilizing" the individual, of in fact corrupting him, working to increase
the numbers of the deracinated [1] and to become the
architect of revolts.

We find ourselves at a loss when confronted by
native law and customs. It is impossible to distinguish what is commendable from what is pernicious
for lack of any criterion to enable us to keep not only
some good things in native custom, but all that is
good therein, cutting out all that is evil. Indeed, there
is a reason for safeguarding, for protecting with every
care, for purifying and refining everything that is
worthy of respect in native custom, in order to make
a link, or, if the metaphor be preferred, a bridgehead,
by means of which natives can attain without hin-

---

1. *Deracinated* : Fr. *déracinés*, those who have been torn
away from their ethnic roots : and who, belonging nowhere,
are very liable as a result of their insecurity to all kinds of
unstable behaviour. (C.K.)

drance all that we have to offer them in respect of stable, deep, true civilization. Only if we set out from the true, the good and the stable in native custom shall we be able to lead our Africans in the direction of a true Bantu civilization.

The fact is that those in high positions do not know to which patron saint to turn for guidance in directing the Bantu, who are growing ever more and more unstable politically. They realize their own impotence to give sound directions worthy of acceptance to ensure the evolution and civilization of the Bantu. All this seems to me to be due to the fact that we have taken no account of Bantu ontology; that we have not as yet succeeded in reproducing syntheses of their thought; and that in consequence we are not fit to judge them upon their ideas.

It has repeatedly been said that evangelization and catechetical work should be adapted... Adapted to what ? We can build churches in native architecture, introduce African melodies into the liturgy, use styles of vestments borrowed from Mandarins or Bedouins, but real adaptation consists in the adaptation of our spirit to the spirit of these people. I shall have occasion to recur to this point. I hope in due course to submit for consideration a catechism adapted to primitive mentality [1].

---

1. "Catéchèse Bantoue" : Les Questions Missionnaires : Abbaye de St. André, Bruges, Belgium.

4. *The gulf dividing Africans and Whites will remain
and widen so long as we do not meet them in the
wholesome aspirations of their own ontology* [1].

Why does not the African change ? How is it that
the pagan, the uncivilized, is stable, while the *évolué*,
the Christian, is not ? Because the pagan founds his
life upon the traditional groundwork of his theodicy
and his ontology, which include his whole mental life
in their purview and supply him with a complete
solution to the problem of living. On the other hand,
the *évolué*, and often the Chrishian, has never effect-
ed a reconciliation between his new way of life and
his former native philosophy, which remains intact
just below the surface (of his behaviour), though we
have rejected it *in toto*, together with the (ensuing)
tribal customs that we misunderstand and disapprove.
This philosophy was, however, the characteristic fea-
ture which made the Bantu the man he was. It

---

1. "I wish to draw attention to the attitude of mind in which
you claim recognition of the full worth of the Black race ("race
noire" C.K.). The point of view which you adopt in regard to
it evokes my wormest congratulations and I am quite sure
that—as so many distinguished persons attest—the fruits of
your work will be a notable advance in racial understanding,
esteem and sympathy, which, by God's will, should unite the
peoples of all countries, regardless of the races to which they
belong."

Dom Pierre Célestin Lou Tseng Tsiang, O.S.B.

belonged to his essential nature. To abandon it amounts to intellectual suicide for him. It should have been our prime task to add new nobility to this Bantu thought.

Need we, then, be surprised that beneath the veneer of "civilization" the "Negro" remains always ready to break through ? We are astonished to find one who has spent years among Whites readapt himself easily by the end of a few months to the community life of his place of origin and soon become reabsorbed in it. He has no need to readjust himself because the roots of his thought are unchanged. Nothing and nobody have made him conscious of any inadequacy in his philosophy.

How many fully civilized persons, or true *évolués*, can we count among the natives of the Congo ? Of *déracinés* and degenerates the number is legion. Of materialists who have lost their foothold in ancestral tradition without having grasped Western thought and philosophy there are not a few. The majority, however, remain "muntu" under a light coating of *white imitation*. Such a one, for example, was a clerk in the Colony whose house was searched during the February 1944 revolt. A note-book was found with magical formulas scribbled from end to end of it ; ...he had copied them in the house of another clerk who had himself transcribed them. In like manner the Elizabethville *évolués* claim, since these revolts, "At last we have found the "magic" way to attain the force of the Whites, while they in future shall have only ours. The Blacks will be henceforth

Whites : the Whites Blacks." These examples show
us clearly how the *évolués* persist in "reasoning"
according to Bantu thought, according to the principle of the interraction of forces.

Whose fault is that ? The fault of the Bantu ?
Perhaps the time has come to make our general
confession ; at any rate, it is time at least to open our
eyes. All of us, missionaries, magistrates, administra-
tors, all in directive posts or posts which ought to be
directive, have failed to reach their "souls", or at any
rate to reach them to the profound degree that should
have been attained. Even specialists have left the
question aside. Whether we state this merely by way
of a frank admission, or avow it with contrition, the
fact remains. By having failed to explore the ontology
of the Bantu, we lack the power to offer them either
a spiritual body of teaching that they are capable of
assimilating, or an intellectual synthesis that they can
understand. By having failed to understand the soul
of the Bantu people, we have neglected to make any
systematic effort to secure for it a purer and a more
dynamic life [1].

It is contended that in condemning the whole
gamut of their supposed "childish and savage customs" by the judgment "this is stupid and bad", we

---

1. Mgr. Van Schingen, Vicar Apostolic of Kwango (Belgian
Congo) writes to me : "I say simply that your pages show those
to be right who, aware of the difficulty of getting at the soul of
the Bantu and of understanding it deeply, have felt constrained
to seek a solid basis of support for their technique of adaptation."

have taken our share of the responsibility for having killed "the man" in the Bantu [1].

We must add, moreover, that it is intellectuals with good will, giving guidance to native society—especially missionaries—who alone can achieve useful work which will contribute to the civilizing of the Bantu. To introduce the Africans to real civilization, much more is necessary than material prosperity, the social welfare that is so much vaunted, and the turning out of ready-made clerks. There must be something more, too, than the teaching of "kifrançais", or English.

In common with so many others, I used to think that we could get rid of Bantu "stupidities" by suitable talks on natural science, hygiene, etc., as if the natural sciences could subvert their traditional lore or their philosophy. We destroy in this way their Natural Sciences, but their fundamental concepts concerning the universe remain unchanged. An example will make this point clear. How many times have we not heard an African accused of being the cause of an illness, even of the death, of some other person simply because he had a dispute with him, or because he had insulted or cursed him ? There is the usual palaver. The accused accepts judgment. He pays the

---

1. It will be shown later that the concrete means by which magic can effectively be fought is not to stifle in the Bantu mind all its native ideas, but to show him that magical practices involve him in contradictions of the healthy principles of his own philosophy.

Fr. "bêtises" : Du. "onnoozelheden" (C.K.).

damages claimed from him, usually without much argument and even, sometimes, in spite of the contrary judgment of an European Court. For the Bantu, indeed, the palaver judgments are clear and indisputable. They have a different conception of the relationships between men, of causality and responsibility. What we regard as the illogical lucubrations of "gloomy Niggers" [1], what we condemn as greed, exploitation of the weak, are for them logical deductions from facts as they see them, and become an ontological necessity. If thereafter we wish to convince Africans of the absurdity of their sizing up of the facts by making them see *how* this man came to fall sick and *of what* he died, that is to say by showing them the *physical causes* of the death or of the illness, we are wasting our time. It would be in vain even to give them a course in microbiology to make them see with their own eyes, or even to discover for themselves through the microscope and by chemical reactions what the "cause" of the death was. Even then we should not have settled *their* problem. We should have decided only the physiological or chemical problem connected with it. The true and underlying cause, the *metaphysical cause*, would none the less remain for them in the terms of their thought, their traditional ontological wisdom. We shall see later how far this point of view is the logical one.

---

1. Fr. "de sombres têtes noires" : Du. "duistere zwarte koppen" (C.K.).

And so the African learns from us to read and
write, to calculate and to do accounts. He becomes
familiar with our techniques ; but, just like his brother who has stayed in the village, he feels through day
to day experience that the lack of comprehension of
the Whites prevents the motivations of his conduct
from being understood. His vital, elemental, traditional lore is wounded. His respect for us and his
confidence in us are in danger of failing under the
test.

5. *Do these fundamental notions and first principles
   really belong to philosophy ?*

In recent decades, the foundation of primitive religion has been successively accepted as consisting in
ancestor worship, animism, cosmic mythology, totemism, magic, until finally it was discovered that
primitive peoples originally had a faith in, and a
worship of, the Supreme Being, the creative Spirit.
All schools of thought have described and studied
African behaviour in the light of their respective
systems. It is striking that these studies have so often
had vague ideas of, approached near to, or even
touched upon, the fundamental concept of Bantu
ontology. Yet we find scarcely any systematic study
of this ontology. No well founded definitions, even,
have been laid down ; in particular, no universally
accepted definitions of animism, totemism, dynamism
and magic. What has been lacking in European in-

3

vestigation, vocabulary, or understanding ? In my opinion, none of these conceptions of primitive thought has been sufficiently exposed to its roots, studied and defined from the point of view of the primitive peoples concerned. How often we find alleged definitions which confine themselves to superficial descriptions of the external aspects of native customs [1].

Why is it that the universal "munganga" (whatever may be the local vernacular variants of the term) is denoted in different authors by such divergent names as sorcerer, fetisher, necromancer, medicine man, magician, etc. ? An exact definition is still to be sought. But the African : in what terms does he think of this personage ? That is the definition which we have to look for.

Admitting that Africans are "animists", in the sense that they locate a "soul" in all beings ; or that we may hold them to be "dynamists" in the sense that they recognise a "mana", an universal force, animating all the beings of the universe, even so we must ask the Bantu themselves the questions, "How can these souls, or this force, be *able*, as you say, to act upon beings ? How does this interaction with beings *take place* ? How can the "bwanga" (magical medicine, amulet, talisman) heal a man, as you say it

---

1. A short time after the Liberation, a colleague brought me from Europe a copy of Westermann : "The African Today and Tomorrow", 2nd Edition, Essen. I had the very agreeable surprise of finding in it the fundamental principles of my theory of forces.

does ? How can the mfwisti, the muloji, the caster of spells, kill you, even at a distance ? How can a dead man be reborn ? What do you understand by this rebirth ? How can the initiation ceremony turn a simple human being into a munganga, a magician healer, or, as we make him to appear later on, a master of forces ? Who initiates, the man or the spirit ? How does the initiate acquire "knowledge" and "power" ? Why does a malediction have a destructive effect ? How is it acquired ? Why is it that our catachumens on the eve of baptism come to us and say : "No doubt our magical cures are potent, but we wish to forswear recourse to them" ?

Such questions go beyond the usual superficial descriptions of native customs. They are not, however, fated to remain for ever unanswered. The answer to them is the one that all Bantu will make without exception. What has been called magic, animism, ancestor-worship, or dynamism—in short, all the customs of the Bantu—depend upon a single principle, knowledge of the Inmost Nature of beings, that is to say, upon their Ontological Principle. For is it not by means of this philosophical term that we must express *their knowledge of being,* of the existence of things ?

6. *Can we give Bantu thought a "philosophical system" ?*

It is universally admitted that humanity evolves.

The Bantu among whom we are living are not completely primitive people. They have evolved. It is
certain that their religion, especially, has done so.
Their customs, habits, behaviour must also have
developed.

It has been claimed that the origin of primitive
religion is to be found in ancestor-worship, animism,
totemism, or magic. According to the most recent
historical research it seems to be established that the
worship of the Suprem Being is at least as old as, if
not older than, magic. Must we, then, conclude that
the Bantu have been successively monotheists, then
animists, and after that totemists ? That they have,
on each occasion, *changed* their religion ? Must one
admit that the changes in religion have been the
result of revolutions ? Is it not more likely that these
modifications of religious conceptions have been the
result of a porgressive evolution from primitive religious days ? This question does not seem to admit of
dispute : what took place was evolution, not revolu-
tion.

Here is the best proof of this thesis. Bantu of the
present day have maintained their faith in what were
originally theistic elements of their religion, yet we
see them today at one and the same time ancestor-
worshippers, animists, dynamists, totemists and
believers in magic. But more : anyone today can
easily verify for himself that our living Bantu say,
speaking of ancestor-worship, animism, etc. "all that
is willed by God, the Supreme Being, and it has all
been given to help us men."

After that can one claim any longer that with each change in religious practices the Bantu changed their mental outlook, modifying their system of thought and their conceptions of the world ? And if, on the contrary, we find these different practices in being side by side, are we then to venture to say that the Bantu have attained to six or seven parallel philosophical systems ? We must do nothing of the sort, but reasonably allow that these different manifestations of faith are linked to one single concept, to one and the same idea of the universe, to one and the same metaphysical principle.

All these religious practices—as elsewhere their juristic conceptions and the political organisation of their society—constitute but one logical whole in the thought of the Bantu. These different realities they explain and justify in relation to their philosophy, a single system and unique to them, their Bantu ontology.

It is not our aim to trace the origins or development of Bantu thought. Neither is it our present business to pass judgment upon the intrinsic worth of their philosophy. Let us for the present refrain from all such judgments, keeping only to ethnology. Let us try above all to *understand* Bantu philosophy, to know what their beliefs are and what is their rational interpretation of the nature of visible and invisible things. These views may be held to be sound or erroneous : in either case we should admit that their ideas on the nature of the universe are essentially metaphysical knowledge, which constitutes them an ontology.

Before we set about teaching these Africans our system of philosophical thought, let us try to master theirs. Without philosophical insight, ethnology is mere folklore... we can no longer be content with vague terms like "the mysterious forces in beings", "certain beliefs", "undefinable influences", or "a certain conception of man and nature". Such definitions, void of all content, have precisely no scientific significance.

We do not claim, of course, that the Bantu are capable of formulating a philosophical treatise, complete with an adequate vocabulary. It is our job to proceed to such systematic development. It is we who will be able to tell them, in precise terms, what their inmost concept of being is. They will recognize themselves in our words and will acquiesce, saying, "You understand us : you now know us completely : you "know" in the way we "know".

More than that, if we can adapt our teaching of true religion to what is worthy of respect in their ontology, we shall hear, in the same way in which it was given to me, such testimony as was given to me. "Now you deceive yourself no longer, you speak as our fathers speak, it always seemed to us that we must be right." They were feeling, I have no doubt, that my instruction, while rejecting the false conclusions of their philosophy, was adapting itself wonderfully to some "soul of truth" in their own fundamental concepts.

7. *Last introductory remarks.*

This present introduction was written only after the completion of my systematic study of Bantu ontology and after my synthesis of their philosophy and its application to our own religious doctrines and catechetical instruction.

It replies to the arguments and criticisms of my colleagues who have been kind enough to interest themselves in these studies and in my exposition of Bantu ontology. It is the result of discussions that have often been very lively. Thanks to their criticisms, I have been able to elaborate this so as to meet certain objections which, though leading to no fruitful issue, would, without this introduction, inevitably arise in the minds of many readers. In developing this preliminary thesis, I have sought to prepare and ease the way for what follows. I confidently hope to be able to convince my readers that real philosophy can be found among indegenous peoples and that it should be sought among them. Many people have already written to me "That is exactly what I have always thought" [1].

---

1. Many colonials living in contact with Africans have assured me that I have set out nothing new, but merely set out systematically what they had grasped vaguely from their practical knowledge of Africans.

The problem of Bantu ontology, the problem whether it exists or not, is thus open to discussion. It is legitimate now to enter upon the task of setting out their philosophy, which is perhaps that common to all primitive peoples, to all clan societies [1].

---

1. Prof. Melville J. Herskovits, of the Northwestern University, Evanston, Illinois, U.S.A., writes : "I am interested that so many of the ideas that Father Tempels exposes as coming from the Belgian Congo are so close to those that I have found among the Sudanese peoples of the Guinea coasts area. They are also the same ideas that we have found in such areas as Haiti and Brazil and Surinam in the New World."

Jean Capart, the Egyptologist, has written : "I have spoken about the Bantu philosophy to those associated with me and read to them Fr. Tempels' little book. I have promised myself a rereading of it and of the "Elements of Negro Customary Law" (by E. Pussoz) for I have an idea, through my first contact with them, that I shall find in them the key to many Egyptian problems. It is often a mistake to begin the study of ancient civilizations by relating them to our own, and by seeking to measure them by unsuitable standards. The concept of LIFE alone allows the Egyptian religion to be assessed at its full worth; and the removal from it of the parasitical excrescences which arouse unfavourable impressions and give rise to harsh judgments."

CHAPTER II

BANTU ONTOLOGY

1. *The terminology used.*

Before beginning to set out the philosophy of the Bantu, we must justify the use of the terms which we shall employ. By so doing we shall forestall certain objections.

Since we are going to treat philosophy, we should use the philosophical terminology accessible to the European reader. As the thought of the Bantu is foreign to ours, we shall call theirs provisionally "the philosophy of magic", though our terminology will not, perhaps, fully cover their thought. Our terms can furnish only an approximation to concepts and principles foreign to us.

Even if we were to employ a literal translation of Bantu terms, we should have to explain to the uninitiated reader the exact force of these native expressions.

We shall, therefore, use English terminology, specifying on every occasion the limitations or extensions by which the received meaning of the terms should be qualified in order to express the Bantu concept exactly.

If our terminology, in spite of this precaution, seems inadequate to the reader, we invite him to suggest an alternative, so that with the benefit of his collaboration, we can approach more nearly to perfection.

The present study, after all, claims to be no more than an *hypothesis,* a first attempt at the systematic development of what Bantu philosophy is. It is necessary to distinguish two quite distinct elements in it :

1) the analysis of Bantu philosophy as I see it ;

2) the terminology in which I have tried to make it accessible to the European reader.

Therefore, even if this terminology should appear inadequate, it should not be concluded that the object of the study itself, an analysis of Bantu thought, is thereby vitiated. I ask the reader to bend his best attention to the essential problem, *the study of Bantu thought,* rather than to boggle over the minor question of terminology.

2. *Method.*

What is the best way in which to set out a systematic exposition of Bantu philosophy while justifying the objectivity of our hypothesis ? We have, in fact, to show the cohesion of our theoretical proposals, while at the same time proving that they are sound, and that they apply to the actualities of Bantu life.

We could begin by a comparative study of the languages, modes of behaviour, institutions and customs of the Bantu ; we could analyse them and separate their fundamental ideas ; finally we could construct from these elements a system of Bantu thought.

This, as a matter of fact, is the method that I followed myself. But it is the long, tedious way of groping and searching, of conceiving an idea and soon afterwards rejecting it ; in which apparent gleams of light lead only back into darkness. It is a story without end, or one which only at long last results in precise, well-defined ideas fitting into a logical system.

This long way, moreover, is not always available to the European reader. It presupposes a long residence among a primitive people, through which, very slowly and without their becoming conscious of it, intimate human contact is established. One lives their life with them, sharing their difficulties, their feasts, their games, their hunting, their palavers. Speaking their language, one learns more by listening to their intercourse one with another than by pursuing systematic investigations. In the end, without knowing how, one attains the ability to think like the Bantu and to look upon life as they do. One is recognised by them as one of themselves, as genuinely Bantu, by reason of one's having come to understand their wisdom. This kind of understanding proves to be far more a matter of experience and of intuition than of study.

For the rest, I have found out only too well that even when one has got to earth with a problem by a study of relevant customs, words and institutions, one easily comes a fatal cropper by falling into argument concerning its details. Customs have, in fact, besides their fundamental significance, a significance which they derive as local colour. Examples which one would cite are always being rejected on grounds such as : "with us this custom is different", or "in our part of the country people express themselves differently".

It therefore seems to me preferable first to present as briefly as possible my complete formulation of Bantu philosophy. After this systematic theoretical exposition, examples from native ways of expressing themselves, or of behaviour which support my theses, will find their place. If the applications of this view of Bantu philosophy yield a satisfactory explanation of observed facts, we way find therein a proof of the validity, even of the exactitude, of our assumptions.

It is true that those who have read my thesis in its early stages have immediately set out certain objections, either against the theories advanced in themselves, or against the terminology used, but always because they were looking at it from the European point of view. Studying with them subsequently innumerable instances of its pratical exemplification in behaviour, I have generally brought the objectors to admit that Bantu philosophy must be something like what I have set it out to be. As for the terminology used, which is generally upsetting at first sight, it has as a rule been conceded to me that it is difficult to find in the philosophical vocabulary of European language terms which cover Bantu thought better.

It seems to me that neither the imperfections of terminology, nor the lacunae which still remain in my suggested synthesis of Bantu philosophy, ought to cause me to hold up publication of the fruits of my investigations and of the conclusions which result from them. May what I now publish result in other scholars being stirred to pursue their own enquiries, so that by collaboration definitive results may be obtained.

I therefore invite the reader of this study to put out of his mind while reading it both his western philosophical thought and any judgments which he may have already made concerning Bantu and primitive peoples. I ask him to abandon received ideas and to apply his mind to getting hold of the significance of what is here said, trying to grasp Bantu thought from within and not allowing himself to be diverted into criticism of my way of setting it out or of my choice of terms. I ask him even to reserve judgment concerning the evaluation to be put upon the theory and, before he pronounces judgment upon it, to have patience to consider the proofs and applications of it which will ultimately be given. After that he may propound his criticisms and attack either the theory itself or the way in which it is set out.

Let us do as the Africans do. When they hold a palaver it is a rule that whoever is arguing a case should suffer an interruption. Even when he stops speaking, the judge will say to him, "Have you finished speaking ?" ; and only after that gives the floor to the opposing side.

3. *Bantu behaviour : it is centred in a single value : vital force* [1].

Certain words are constantly being used by Africans. They are those which express their supreme values ; and they recur like variations upon a *leitmotif* present in their language, their thought, and in all their acts and deeds.

This suprem value is *life, force, to live strongly,* or *vital force.*

The Bantu say, in respect of a number of strange practices in which we see neither rime nor reason, that their purpose is to acquire *life, strength* or *vital force, to live strongly,* that they are to make life

---

1. See note on Terminology, p. 8. The French terms are *la force, vivre fort, force vitale.* Despite precedents, I am still affronted by the phrase "vital force"; but if the reader, equally jarred, is driven in his search fo ran alternative to ponder the whole context of the concept involved in Fr. Tempels'book, he may in the end conclude that his time has not been ill-spent. (C.K.)

stronger, or to assure that force shall remain perpetually in one's posterity.

Used negatively, the same idea is expressed when the Bantu say : we act thus to be protected from misfortune, or from a diminution of life or of being, or in order to protect ourselves from those influences which annihilate or diminish us.

Force, the *potent life, vital energy* are the object of prayers and invocations to God, to the spirits and to the dead, as well as of all that is usually called magic, sorcery or magical remedies. The Bantu will tell you that they go to a diviner to learn the words of life, so that he can teach them the way of making life stronger. In every Bantu language it is easy to recognize the words or phrases denoting a *force,* which is not used in an exclusively bodily sense, but in the sense of the integrity of our whole being.

The *bwanga* (which has been translated "magical remedy") ought not, they say, to be applied to the wound or sick limb. It does not necessarily possess local therapeutic effects, but it strengthens, it increases the vital force.

In calling upon God, the spirits, or the ancestral spirits, the heathen ask above all, "give me force". If one urges them to abandon magical practices, as being contrary to the will of God and therefore evil, one will get the reply, "wherein are they wicked ?" What we brand as magic is, in their eyes, nothing but setting to work natural forces placed at the disposal of man by God to strengthen man's vital energy.

When they try to get away from metaphors and

periphrases, the Bantu speak of God himself as "the Strong One", he who possesses Force in himself. He is also the source of the Force of every creature. God is the "Dijina dikatampe" : the great name, because he is the great Force, the "mukomo", as our Baluba have it, the one who is stronger than all others [1].

The spirits of the first ancestors, highly exalted in the superhuman world, possess extraordinary force inasmuch as they are the founders of the human race and propagators of the divine inheritance of vital human strength. The other dead are esteemed only to the extent to which they increase and perpetuate their vital force in their progeny.

In the minds of Bantu, all beings in the universe possess vital force of their own : human, animal, vegetable, or inanimate. Each being has been endowed by God with a certain force, capable of strengthening the vital energy of the strongest being of all creation : man.

Supreme happiness, the only kind of blessing, is, to the Bantu, to possess the greatest vital force : the worst misfortune and, in very truth, the only misfortune, is, he thinks, the diminution of this power.

Every illness, wound or disappointment, all suffering, depression, or fatigue, every injustice and every failure : all these are held to be, and are spoken of by the Bantu as, a diminution of vital force.

Illness and death do not have their source in our own vital power, but result from some external agent

---

1. Fr. "Le Puissant" (C.K.).

who weakens us through his greater force. It is only by fortifying our vital energy, through the use of magical recipes, that we acquire resistance to malevolent external forces.

We need not be surprised that the Bantu allude to this vital force in their greetings one to another, using such forms of address as : "You are strong", or "you have life in you", "you have life strongly in you" ; and that they express sympathy in such phrases as "your vital force is lowered", "your vital energy has been sapped". A similar idea is found in the form of sympathy, "wafwa ko !" which we translate "you are dying" ; and by reason of our mistranslation, we are quite unable to understand the Bantu and find them given to ridiculous exaggeration when they continually say that they are "dead" of hunger or of fatigue, or that the least obstacle or illness is "killing" them. In their own minds they are simply indicating a diminution of vital force, in which sense their expression is reasonable and sensible enough. In their languages, too, are words like "kufwa" and "fukwididila", indicating the progressing stages of loss of force, of vitality, and the superlative of which signifies total paralysis of the power to live. It is quite erroneous for us to translate these words by "to die" and "to die entirely".

This explains what has, indeed, been true, that the thing which most inhibits pagans from conversion to Christianity and from giving up magical rites is the fear of attenuating this vital energy through ceasing to have recourse to the natural powers which sustain it.

In 1936 I gave my Normal Class students at Lukonzolwa (Lake Moëro) as an essay subject, "Obstacles to conversion among pagan peoples". To my astonishment, so far from setting out a list of practices, all of them declared that the great obstacle could be summed up in a conviction that to abandon the customs appointed by their ancestors would lead to death. The objection, therefore, was rather a matter of principle than of practice, their fear being grounded in the "truths" of Bantu ontology.

These various aspects of Bantu behaviour already enable us to see that the key to Bantu thought is the idea of vital force, of which the source is God[1].

---

1. The Revd. Sister Carmela, of the Sœurs Missionnaires de Notre Dame d'Afrique supplies important confirmation from Bunia, in Ituri (Belgian Congo) : "... Here the African never speaks of "vital force". When anyone speaks to him about it, he replies, "Yes, it is exactly like that with us"; and he smiles with satisfaction. And they say one to another, "She knows us".

But among them the facts are such that everyone knows them and nobody needs to talk about them. For example, they say, we never speak of the "force of life" because with us life and force are one and the same thing. If one is less strong, one does not speak of life. Neither does one say that life "is becoming stronger"; one feels it; one has an impression of it.

And, if favourable external conditions make you stronger, it will be said that you have power...

Evidently vital force is to the African mind the great and important thing.

They have also some small idea of being, but as some quite higher thing. For example, a woman reflecting upon injustice on the part of a stronger party : "God is". She does not say "God lives!" Since our Africans are unable to obtain justice they say, "God is!"

Vital force is the reality which, though invisible, is supreme in man. Man can renew his vital force by tapping the strength of other creatures.

4. *Bantu ontology.*

a) The general notion of being[1].

We have seen that the Bantu soul hankers after life and force. The fundamental notion under which being is conceived lies within the category of forces.

Metaphysics studies this reality, existing in everything and in every being in the universe. It is in virtue of this reality that all beings have something in common, so that the definition of this reality may be applied to all existent forms of being.

To arrive at this reality common to all beings, or rather, which is identical in all beings, it is necessary to eliminate all forms of reality which belong to one category only among beings.

The Bahema, Alur, Walenda all have the same philosophy as the Bantu. The forms of religion change, yes; but the basis of it is exactly the same."

1. "The chief value of your book consists, I think, in your demonstration of the difference which exists between Africans and Whites in the way in which they conceive of being. That is a fine discovery indeed, the fruit of your penetrating and patient analysis, which deserves all praise. It constitutes a contribution of which we must take full account in order the better to enter into African thought and the better to understand them. On this point your work seems to me to be impressive beyond any possibility of contradiction." Achille, Card. Lienart.

We pay attention to the elements only, but to all the elements which are common to all beings. Such elements are, e.g. the origin, the growth, the changes, the destruction, or the achievement of the beings, passive and active causality, and particularly the nature of the being as such supporting those universal phenomena. These elements constitute the object of metaphysical knowledge, that is to say, of knowledge embracing all the physical or the real.

Metaphysics does not treat of the abstract or the unreal : these are but its notions, its definitions, its laws, which are abstract and general, as the notions, definitions and laws of every science always are.

Christian thought in the West, having adopted the terminology of Greek philosophy and perhaps under its influence, has defined this reality common to all beings, or, as one should perhaps say, being as such ; "the reality that is", "anything that exists", "what is". Its metaphysics has most generally been based upon a fundamentally *static* conception of being.

Herein is to be seen the fundamental difference between Western thought and that of the Bantu and other primitive people. (I compare only systems which have inspired widespread "civilizations").

We can conceive the transcendental notion of "being" by separating it from its attribute, "Force", but the Bantu cannot. "Force" in his thought is a necessary element in "being", and the concept "force" is inseparable from the definition of "being". There is no idea among Bantu of "being" divorced from the idea of "force". Without the element "force", "being" cannot be conceived.

We hold a *static* conception of "being", they a *dynamic*.

What has been said above should be accepted as the basis of Bantu ontology : in particular, *the concept "force" is bound to the concept "being" even in the most abstract thinking upon the notion of being.*

At least it must be said that the Bantu have a double concept concerning being, a concept which can be expressed : "being is that which has force".

But I think we must go further. Our statement of Bantu philosophy should press as closely as possible its distinctive characteristics. It seems to me that we shall not attain this precision by formulating the notion of being *in Bantu thought* as "*being* is that which *possesses* force".

I believe that we should most faithfully render the Bantu thought in European language by saying that Bantu speak, act, live as if, for them, beings were forces. Force is not for them an adventitious, accidental reality. Force is even more than a necessary attribute of beings : *Force is the nature of being, force is being, being is force* [1].

---

1. It can rightly be said that the Bantu regard being as exclusively or essentially a "principle of activity". This term is borrowed from our scientific and therefore more philosophical terminology. One must on that account be careful not to understand it in relation to our static concepts of being, but in accordance with Bantu thought wherein this same principle is regarded as realising itself more or less in itself.

When we think in terms of the concept "being", they use the concept "force". Where we see concrete beings, they see concrete forces. When we say that "beings" are differentiated by their essence or nature, Bantu say that "forces" differ in their essence or nature. They hold that there is the divine force, celestial or terrestrial forces, human forces, animal forces, vegetable and even material or mineral forces.

The reader will be able to form his own opinion at the end of this study as to the validity, the exact worth of this hypothesis : *in contradistinction to our definition of being as "that which is", or "the thing insofar as it is", the Bantu definition reads, "that which is force", or "the thing insofar as it is force", or "an existent force".* We must insist once again that "force" is not for Bantu a necessary, irreducible attribute of being : no, the notion "force" takes for them the place of the notion "being" in our philosophy. Just as we have, so have they a transcendental, elemental, simple concept : with them "force", with us "being".

It is because all being is force and exists only in that it is force, that the category "force" includes of necessity all "beings" : God, men living and departed, animals, plants, minerals. Since being is force, all these beings appear to the Bantu as forces. This universal concept is hardly used by the Bantu, but they are susceptible to philosophical abstractions though they express them in concrete terms only. They give a name to each thing, but the inner life of these things presents itself to their minds as such specific forces and not at all as static reality [1].

It would be a misuse of words to call the Bantu "dynamists" or "energists", as if the universe were animated by some universal force, a sort of unique magical power encompassing all existence, as certain authors seem to believe, judging from their treatment of "mana", "bwanga", or "kanga". Such is an European presentation of a primitive philosophy that is but imperfectly understood. The Bantu make a clear distinction and understand an essential difference between different beings, that is to say, different forces. Among the different kinds of forces they have come to recognize, just as we do, unity, individuality but individuality clearly understood as meaning individuality of forces [2].

That is why it seems to me necessary to reject as foreign to Bantu philosophy the dualism of good and evil as two forces ; and also what has been called "common being" or "community of nature", when these terms are so used as to eliminate the individuality of forces.

In the category of visible beings the Bantu distin-

---

1. A missionary to the Ubangi (Belgian Congo) writes to me : "My researches in linguistics confirm in my mind how universally African your study is. Among the Ngbaka the "substantive" indicates a thing less as "that" than as "thus". We contemplate the "being" of the thing, they its "force". It is the extent, more or less, to which a thing is vital force that constitutes for them the "being" of the thing."

2. The Du. reads, "units or individuals standing by themselves, each of them being a force apart." (C.K.)

guish that which is perceived by the senses and the
"thing in itself". By the "thing in itself" they indicate
its individual inner nature, or, more precisely, the
force of the thing. They are expressing themselves in
figurative language when they say "in every thing
there is another thing ; in every man a little man".
But one would grossly deceive oneself in wishing to
attribute to this piece of imagery any exact verbal
expression of the Bantu notion of being. Their alleg-
ory merely brings into relief the distinction they make
between the contingent, the visible phenomenon of
being or of force, and the intrinsic visible nature of
that force.

When "we" differentiate in man the soul and the
body, as is done in certain Western writings, we are
at a loss to explain where "the man" has gone after
these two components have been separated out. If,
from our European outlook, we wish to seek Bantu
terms adequate to express this manner of speaking,
we are up against very great difficulties, especially if
we are proposing to speak about the soul of man.
Unless under European influence, the Bantu do not
thus express themselves. They distinguish in man
body, shadow and breath. This breath is the assumed
manifestation, the evident sign of life, though it is
mortal and in no way corresponds with what we
understand by the soul, especially the soul as subsis-
ting after death, when the body with its shadow and
its breath will have disappeared. What lives on after
death is not called by the Bantu by a term indicating
part of a man. I have always heard their elders speak

of "the man himself", "himself", aye mwine" ; or it
is "the little man" who was formerly hidden behind
the perceptible manifestation of the man ; or the
"muntu", which, at death, has left the living.

It seems to me incorrect to translate this word
"muntu" by "the man". The "muntu" certainly possesses a visible body, but this body *is not* the "muntu". A Bantu one day explained to one of my colleagues that the " muntu" is rather what you call in
English the "person" and not what you connote by
"the man". "Muntu" signifies, then, vital force, endowed with intelligence and will. This interpretation
gives a logical meaning to the statement which I one
day received from a Bantu : "God is a great muntu"
("Vidye i muntu mukatampe"). This meant "God is
the great Person" ; that is to say, *The* great, powerful
and reasonable living force.

The "bintu" are rather what we call *things* ; but
according to Bantu philosophy they are beings, that
is to say *forces not endowed with reason, not living.*

b) All force can be strengthened or enfeebled.
    That is to say, all being can become stronger or
    weaker.

We say of a man that he grows, develops, acquires
knowledge, exercises his intelligence and his will ;
and that in so doing he increases them. We do not
hold that by these acquisitions and by this development he has become more a man ; at least, not in the

sense that his human *nature* no longer remains what it was. One either has human nature or one hasn't. It is not a thing that is increased or diminished. Development operates in a man's qualities or in his faculties.

Bantu ontology—or, to be more exact, the Bantu theory of forces—is radically opposed to any such conception. When a Bantu says "I am becoming stronger", he is thinking of something quite different from what we mean when we say that our powers are increasing. Remember that, for the Bantu, being is force and force being. When he says that a force is increasing, or that a being is reinforced, his thought must be expressed in our language and according to our mental outlook as "this being has grown as such", his nature has been made stronger, increased, made greater. What Catholic theology teaches concerning, in particular, the supernatural realities of grace, that it is a supernal reinforcement of our being, that it is able to grow and to be strengthened in itself, is an idea similar to what the Bantu accept in the natural order as true of all being, of all force.

This is the sense in which it seems that we should understand the expressions which have been quoted to show that the behaviour of the Bantu is centred on the idea of vital energy : "to be strong", "to reinforce your life", "you are powerful", "be strong" ; or again, "your vital force is declining, has been affected".

It is in this sense also that we must understand

Fraser, when he writes in the "Golden Bough", "The soul like the body can be fat or thin, great or small" ; or again, "the diminution of the shadow is considered to be the index of a parallel enfeeblement in the vital energy of its owner" [1].

The same idea again is envisaged by M. E. Possoz when he writes in his "Elements of Negro Customary Law" : "For the African, existence is a thing of variable intensity" ; and further on when he mentions "the diminution or the reinforcement of being".

We must speak next of the existence of things or of forces. The origin, the subsistence or annihilation of beings or of forces, is expressly and exclusively attributed to God. The term "to create" in its proper connotation of "to evoke from not being" is found in its full signification in Bantu terminology (kupanga in Kiluba). It is in this sense that the Bantu see, in the phenomenon of conception, a direct intervention of God in creating life.

Those who think that, according to the Bantu, one being can entirely annihilate another, to the point that he ceases to exist, conceive a false idea. Doubtless one force that is greater than another can paralyse it, diminish it, or even cause its operation totally to cease, but for all that the force does not cease to exist. Existence which comes from God cannot be taken from a creature by any created force.

---

1. The references are to pp. 179 and 191 of the abridged 1 vol. edition· (C.K.)

  c) The interaction of forces : one being influenc-
     ing another.

We speak of the mechanical, chemical and psychi-
cal interactions between beings. Realists and idealists
meet in recognizing yet another causality conditioning
being itself, the cause of the existence of being as
such. It is a metaphysical causality which binds the
creature to the Creator. The relationship of the creature to the Creator is a constant. I mean to say that
the creature is by his nature permanently dependent
upon his Creator for existence and means of survival.
We do not conceive of any equivalent relationship
between creatures. Created beings are denoted in
Scholastic philosophy as substances, that is to say,
beings who exist, if not by themselves, at any rate in
themselves, *in se, non in alio*. The child is, from
birth, a new being, a complete human being. It has
the fulness of human nature and its human existence
as such is independent of that of its progenitors. The
human nature of a child does not remain in permanent causal relationship with that of its parents.
  This concept of separate beings, of substance (to
use the Scholastic term again) which find themselves
side by side, entirely independent one of another, is
foreign to Bantu thought. Bantu hold that created
beings preserve a bond one with another, an intimate
ontological relationship, comparable with the causal
tie which binds creature and Creator. For the Bantu
there is interaction of being with being, that is to say,
of force with force. Transcending the mechanical,

chemical and psychological interactions, they see a relationship of forces which we should call ontological. In the *created force* (a contingent being) the Bantu sees a causal action emanating from the very nature of that created force and influencing other forces. One force will reinforce or weaken another. This causality is in no way supernatural in the sense of going beyond the proper attributes of created nature. It is, on the contrary, a metaphysical causal action which flows out of the very nature of a created being. General knowledge of these activities belongs to the realm of natural knowledge and constitutes *philosophy* properly so called. The observation of the action of these forces in their specific and concrete applications would constitute Bantu natural science.

This interaction of beings has been denoted by the word "magic". If it is desired to keep the term, it must be modified so that it is understood in conformity with the content of Bantu thought. In what Europeans call "primitive magic" there is, to primitive eyes, no operation of supernatural, indeterminate forces, but simply the interaction between natural forces, as they were created by God and as they were put by him at the disposal of men.

In their studies of magic, authors distinguish "imitative magic", "sympathetic magic", "contagious magic", "magic of expressed desire", etc. Whatever the resemblance, contact, or the expression of desire, does not arise out of the essence of what is indicated by magic, that is to say, the interaction of creatures.

The very fact that there should have been recourse to different terms to distinguish the "kinds"[1] of magic, proves that any attempt to penetrate to the real nature of magic has been given up in favour of a classification in terms of secondary characters only.

The child, even the adult, remains always for the Bantu a man, a force, in causal dependence and ontological subordination to the forces which are his father and mother. The older force ever dominates the younger. It continues to exercise its living influence over it. This is said to give a first example of the Bantu conception in accordance with which the "beings-forces" of the universe are not a multitude of independent forces placed in juxtaposition from being to being. All creatures are found in relationship according to the laws of a hierarchy that I shall describe later. Nothing moves in this universe of forces without influencing other forces by its movement. The world of forces is held like a spider's web of which no single thread can be caused to vibrate without shaking the whole network.

It has been maintained that "beings" only acquire "power" to act upon other beings or forces through the intervention of spirits and manes. This contention emanates from European observers, it does not exist

---

1. Fr. "espèces" (inverted commas in the original). The word is used in two senses : *a*) referring to the different "kinds" of magic named by older anthropologists and quoted above; *b*) indicating that these "kinds" are in truth manifestations or "appearances" only of the inadequately conceived reality underlying magic of all kinds. (C.K.)

in the minds of Africans. The dead intervene on
occasion to *make* known to the living the nature and
quality of certain forces, but they do not thereby
change that nature or those qualities which are preor-
dained as belonging to that force. Africans expressly
say that creatures *are* forces, created by God as
such ; and that the intervention of spirits or manes
changes nothing : such changes are a White man's
idea.

d) The hierarchy of forces : primogeniture.

As with Indian castes and as the Israelites distinguished the "pure" from the "impure", so beings are
differentiated in Bantu ontology into species according to their vital power ("levenskracht") or their
inherent vital rank ("levensrang"). Above all force is
God, Spirit and Creator, the *mwine bukomo bwandi.*
It is he who has force, power, in himself. He gives
existence, power of survival and of increase, to other
forces. In relation to other forces, he is "He who
increases force" [1]. After him come the first fathers
of men, founders of the different clans. These archi-
patriarchs were the first to whom God communicated
his vital force, with the power of exercising their
influences on all posterity. They constitute the most
important chain binding men to God. They occupy so

1. Du. "versterker".

exalted a rank in Bantu thought that they are not regarded merely as ordinary dead. They are no longer named among the manes ; and by the Baluba they are called *bavidye,* spiritualised beings, beings belonging to a higher hierarchy, participating to a certain degree in the divine Force [1].

After these first parents come the dead of the tribe, following their order of primogeniture. They form a chain, through the links of which the forces of the elders exercise their vitalising influence on the living generation. Those living on earth rank, in fact, after the dead. The living belong in turn to a hierarchy, not simply following legal status, but as ordered by their own being in accordance with primogeniture and their vital rank ; that is to say, according to their vital power.

But man is not suspended in thin air. He lives on his land, where he finds himself to be the sovereign vital force, ruling the land and all that lives on it : man, animal, or plant. The eldest of a group or of a

---

1. The language of the Bantu would cause one to think that they identify the founders of the clan with God himself. It so happens that they call both by the same name. There is, however, no identification, but a simple comparison, a practice analagous to that in which a Chief's deputy is treated as the Chief himself, since he is his sensory manifestation and his speech is often the word of him who sent him.

We often hear an African say to someone who has befriended him : "You are my father and mother, you are my supreme Chief. You are my God." Often, too, Africans have called me "Syakapanga" (Creator). They were in this way expressing their conviction that I was His word-bearer, His messenger to them.

clan is, for Bantu, by Divine law the sustaining link of life, binding ancestors and their descendants. It is he who "reinforces" the life of his people and of all inferior forces, animal, vegetable and inorganic, that exist, grow, or live on the foundation which he provides for the welfare of his people. The true chief, then, following the original conception and political set up of clan peoples, is the father, the master, the king ; he is the source of all zestful living ; he is as God himself. This explains what the Bantu mean when they protest against the nomination of a chief, by government intervention, who is not able, by reason of his vital rank or vital force, to be the link binding dead and living. "Such an one cannot be chief. It is impossible. Nothing would grow in our soil, our women would bear no children and everything would be struck sterile." Such considerations and such despair are entirely mysterious and incomprehensible so long as we have not grasped the Bantu conception of existence and their interpretation of the universe. Judged, however, according to the *theory of forces*, their point of view becomes logical and clear.

After the category of human forces come the other forces, animal, vegetable and mineral. But within each of these categories is found a hierarchy based on vital power, rank and primogeniture.

From that it follows that an analogy can be found between a human and a lower group (e.g. in the animal class), an analogy based on the relative place of these groups in relation to its own class. Such

5

would be an analogy founded on primogeniture or upon a pre-determined order of subordination. A human group and an animal species can occupy in their respective classes a rank relatively equal or relatively different. Their vital rank can be parallel or different. A Chief in the class of humans shows his royal rank by wearing the skin of a royal animal. The respect for this ranking in life, the care not to place oneself higher than one's legitimate place, the necessity not to approach the higher forces as if they were our equals, all that can supply the key to the so much disputed problem of "tabu" and "totem".

e) The Created Universe is centred on man. The present human generation living on earth is the centre of all humanity, including the world of the dead.

The Jews had no precise views of the beyond, nothing more than that of compensation in the future life for earthly merit. The idea of *bliss* became known to them a short time only before the coming of Christ. "Sheol" was a desolate region ; and sojourn there seemed a gloomy business, offering little enough to attract those who had the good fortune to be still living on earth.

In the minds of the Bantu, the dead also live ; but theirs is a diminished life, with reduced vital energy. This seems to be the conception of the Bantu when they speak of the dead in general, superficially and in

regard to the external things of life. When they consider the inner reality of being, they admit that deceased ancestors have not lost their superior reinforcing influence ; and that the dead in general have
acquired a greater knowledge of life and of vital or
natural force. Such deeper knowledge as they have in
fact been able to learn concerning vital and natural
forces they use only to strengthen the life of man on
earth. The same is true of their superior force by
reason of primogeniture, which can be employed only
to reinforce their living posterity. The dead forbear
who can no longer maintain active relationships with
those on earth is "completely dead", as Africans say.
They mean that this individual vital force, already
diminished by decease, has reached a zero diminution
of energy, which becomes completely static through
lack of faculty to employ its vital influence on behalf
of the living. This is held to be the worst of disasters
for the dead themselves. The spirits of the dead
("manes") seek to enter into contact with the living
and to continue living function upon earth.

Inferior forces, on the other hand (animal, plant,
mineral) exist only, and by the will of God, to increase the vital force of men while they are on earth.
Higher and lower forces, therefore, are thought of by
the Bantu in relation to living human forces. For this
reason I have preferred to call the influences of one
created being upon another *causal agencies of life,*
rather than causal agencies of being[1], or of force as

---

1. Du. "liever levesninvloeden dan wesensinvloeden".

we have provisionally termed them. In fact, even
inferior beings, such as inanimate beings and minerals, are forces which by reason of their nature have
been put at the disposal of men, of living human
forces, or of men's vital forces.

The white man, a new phenomenon in the Bantu
world, could be conceived only according to pre-
existing categories of Bantu thought. He was therefore incorporated into the universe of forces, in the
position therein which was congruent with the logic
of Bantu ontology. The technological skill of the
white man impressed the Bantu. The white man
seemed to be the master of great natural forces. It
had, therefore, to be admitted that the white man was
an elder, a superior human force, surpassing the vital
force of all Africans. The vital force of the white man
is such that against it the "manga", or the application
of active natural forces at the disposition of Africans,
was without effect.

f) The General Laws of Vital Causality.

After what we have said upon the question of
"force-beings"[1] grouped in respect of their natures,
of intensity of life class by class, and of the precedence according to primogeniture, it will be now clear
that, among clan peoples, the universe of forces is

---

1. F. "êtres-forces".

organically constructed in what we can call an ontological hierarchy. The interaction of forces and the
exercise of vital influences occurs, in fact, according
to determined laws. The Bantu universe is not a
chaotic tangle of unordered forces blindly struggling
with one another. Nor must we believe that this
theory of forces is the incoherent product of a savage
imagination, or that the action of the same force can
be now propitious and now pernicious, without a
determining power to justify the fact. Doubtless there
are force influences acting in this unforeseeable manner, but this assertion does not allow the conclusion
that action occurs in a manner scientifically unpre-
dictable, in a totally irrational mode. When a motor-
car breaks down, one can say that this event was not
determined in advance by what constitutes the essential nature of a motor-car, but we do not on that
account believe ourselves obliged to deny the correct-
ness and validity of the laws of mechanics. On the
contrary, the breakdown itself can be explained only
by adequate application of these very laws. The same
is true of the laws of the interaction of forces. There
are possible and necessary actions, other influences
are metaphysically impossible by reason of the nature
of the forces in question. The possible causal factors
in life can be formulated in certain metaphysical,
universal, immutable and stable laws.

These laws can, I think, be set out as follows :

I. Man (living or deceased) can directly reinforce
or diminish the being of another man.

Such vital influence is possible from man to man : it is indeed necessarily effective as between the progenitor, a superior vital force —and his progeny—an inferior force. This interaction does not occur only when the recipient object is endowed, in respect of the endowing subject, with a superior force, which he may achieve of himself, or by some vital external influence, or (especially) by the action of God.

II. The vital human force can directly influence inferior force-beings (animal, vegetable, or mineral) in their being itself.

III. A rational being (spirit, manes, or living) can act indirectly upon another rational being by communicating his vital influence to an inferior force (animal, vegetable, or mineral) through the intermediacy of which it influences the rational being. This influence will also have the character of a necessarily effective action, save only when the object is inherently the stronger force, or is reinforced by the influence of some third party, or preserves himself by recourse to inferior forces exceeding those which his enemy is employing.

Note : Certain authors claim that inanimate beings, stones, rocks, or plants and trees are called by the

Bantu "bwanga", as exercising their vital influence on all that comes near them. If this were authenticated, it would open the question : "do lower forces act by themselves upon higher forces ?" Some authors say that they do. For my part, I have never met any African who would accept this hypothesis. *A priori*, such an occurrence would seem to me to contradict the general principles of the theory of forces. In Bantu metaphysic the lower force is excluded from exercising by its own initiative any vital action upon a higher force. Besides, in giving their examples, these authors ought to recognize that often a living influence has been at work, for example, that of the manes. Likewise certain natural phenomena, rocks, waterfalls, big trees, can be considered—and are considered by the Bantu—as manifestations of divine power ; they can also be the sign, the manifestation, the habitat of a spirit. It seems to me that such should be the explanation of the apparent influences of lower forces on the higher force of man. Those lower beings do not exercise their influence of themselves, but through the vital energy of a higher force acting as cause. Such an explanation accords in all cases with Bantu metaphysic. Such manifestations belong to the third law enunciated above.

CHAPTER III

BANTU WISDOM OR CRITERIOLOGY [1]

1. *What is Bantu Wisdom?*

It consists in the Bantu's discernment of the nature of beings, of forces : true wisdom lies in ontological knowledge. The Sage "par excellence" is God, who knows every being, Who comprehends the nature and the quality of the energy of each [2].

God is Force, possessing energy in himself, the mover of all other forces. He knows all forces, their ordering, their dependence, their potential and their mutual interactions. He knows, therefore, the cause of every event. *Vidye uyukile :* God knows. Such is the ultimate reference of the Baluba in face of every insoluble problem, before every inescapable evil ; and

---

1. Criteriology : Du. kennisleer, Fr. criteriologie. See N.E.D. "the doctrine of a criterion (of knowledge, etc.) quoting one example of it from the "Atheneum", 14th July, 1884: "the relation of thought to reality as regards its validity." (C.K.)

2. I abe Shayuka uyuka dyuba ne bufuku : Thou art the Father of knowledge, thou knowest the day and the night.

each time that human wisdom is taken to the court of reason.

In the administration of justice, when all human presumptions agree to crush an innocent litigant deprived of means to prove his case, he will protest : *Vidye uyukile!* God knows : God, who knows every deed and the true man in the intimacy of his being, knows my innocence.

When the *manga,* the magic strengtheners of being, fail, the remedy maker will say *Vidye wakoma,* God is strong[1]. This means : He is stronger than my remedies. But those pagans who, while accepting the principle of vital interactions, do not believe in certain concrete applications or proposed remedies will say, in resigning themselves to an evil, the cause of which is escaping them : Vidye uyukile : God knows (yet he allows it).

Nothing in fact happens without the permission of the Strongest One. The sentence "He knows" certainly means "He understands the occurrence", but it means more often, "He has his reasons".

God knows. He gives man "power" to know. Let us remember that all being is force, that each of its faculties is a force. There is, therefore, the force of knowing, just as there is a force of willing. Therefore men have the power of knowing. There are above all the ancestors, the *ba-vidye,* and among them the

---

1. Du. "wanneer *manga*—"magische" versterkingsmddelen—niet baten zal de *manga*-man zeggen : Vidye wakoma, God is sterk, d.i. sterker dan *mijn manga.*"

elders, dead or living, who know. "It is they who started things".

True knowledge, human wisdom, then, will equally be metaphysical : it will be the intelligence of forces, of their hierarchy, their cohesion and their interaction.

I have stated the primacy of ancestors, the elders. In fact, just as the vital human force (its being) does not exist by itself, but is and remains essentially dependent upon its elders, so the power to know is, like being itself, essentially dependent upon the wisdom of the elders.

How often in a village, when one wishes to question Bantu about some happening—a law suit or a custom, or even some geographical or geological data—does not one provoke the reply : "We younger ones do not know : it is the elders who know." That happens even when the matter in question is, as we think, something which them know all about. Nevertheless, as they think, they do not know, because they are young, because they do not know of or by themselves. Ontologically and juridically the elders who hold the ascendancy are the only ones to know fully, in the last resort. Their wisdom exceeds that of other men. It is in this sense that the old say : "The young cannot know without the elders." "If it were not for the elders," the Bantu say again, "if the young were left to themselves, the village would get nowhere. The young would no longer know how to live : they would have neither customs, laws, nor wisdom any longer. They would stray into disaster."

Study and the personal search for knowledge does not give wisdom. One can learn to read, to write, to count : to manage a motor car, or learn a trade ; but all that has nothing in common with "wisdom". It gives no ontological knowledge of the nature of beings. There are many talents and clever skills that remain far short of wisdom.

That is how the Bantu speak of their traditional wisdom.

Let us now see how Europeans would set out to give a reasoned exposition of Bantu wisdom and of their system of criteriology.

2. *Metaphysics, or the Philosophy of Forces, is within the capacity of every Bantu.*

The philosophy of forces is a theory of life, a *weltanschaung*. It is possible that it may have been devised to justify a given behaviour, or that a particular adaptation of nature may have conditioned this behaviour, but always the philosophy of forces strictly governs in fact the whole of Bantu life.

It explains the human motivations of all Bantu customs. It decrees the norms in accordance with which personality in the individual shall be kept unaltered or allowed to develop [1]. This does not

---

1. Du. "Maar het is toch zeker, dat een *muntu*, die zijn leven niet richt naar algemeene lijnen van de eeuwenoude Bantu filosofie, door de Bantu zelf voor *kidima* uitdemaakt wordt, voor een mensch die niet voldoende verstand bezit om als

mean that every Bantu is able to enumerate the
cardinal truths of his philosophy, but it is not less
true that the "muntu" who neglects to orientate his
life in accordance with the ancient norms laid down
by Bantu wisdom will be treated as "kidima" by his
fellows : that is to say as a sub-human, a man of
insufficient mind to count as a "muntu". The normal
"muntu" knows his philosophy, he recognizes the
forces in beings[1]. He knows about the growth of
beings and their ontological influences. He notes the
operation of the general laws of cause and effect
between living forces which we treated above in the
chapter on Bantu ontology. This ontology, inasmuch
as it remains universal and truly philosophical knowledge, is the common property of the whole Bantu
society. This universal wisdom is accepted by
everyone, it is not subjected to criticism, it has cur-
rency, in regard to its general principles, as imperishable Truth.

The ethnological views which have been set out in
this book do not constitute a secret knowledge con-

---

volledig, normaal mensch door de gaan, dus voor een minus
habens." "This does not mean that every *muntu* can say off-
hand the ten cardinal truths of his philosophy of life, but it is
certain that a *muntu* who does not order his life according to
the general rules of the age old Bantu philosophy will be called
kidima by the Bantu themselves as a man who has not enough
brains to be considered a normal person, therefore as a minus
habens." (C.K.)

1. Better, according to the Du. "beings as forces", "wesens
als krachten". (C.K.)

fined to a few savants or initiates. We have set down
only the popular wisdom of the common man.

3. *Bantu philosophy is based on internal and external evidence.*

If the Bantu so generally accept their present
beliefs free from doubt, that is because—they say—
their wisdom is engendered in them at the same time
as their living force by their parents and ancestors
who continue to instruct them by means of divination. Songs, fables, mythological traditions and
ceremonies of initiation assure instruction in Bantu
thought. However, they draw other arguments from
their own experience. Since their ancestors proceeded
from God himself, should not they have a longer
knowledge than they themselves ? Besides, their
ancestors lived by this philosophy, preserved and
handed down life through their recourse to these
natural forces, and saved the Bantu people from
destruction. Consequently their wisdom seems sound
and sufficient. Moreover, this practical wisdom is so
completely adapted by the elders to the needs of life
that no problem is, so to speak, left unanswered ; and
that a prescription is provided for every eventuality :
this, to the minds of the Bantu, affords proof of the
fundamental and realistic soundness of their philosophy. Thus Mgr. Leroy says in "La Religion des
Primitifs" that the Bantu sees himself engaged in a
constant struggle with the forces of nature which

surround him ; and he emerges from this struggle, now as victor, now as vanquished. He establishes every day the existence of hidden forces in plants and herbs. For primitive minds, these considerations furnish adequate grounds of proof of the validity of their philosophy of forces and of the concept of beings as forces. To see that natural forces are sometimes potent and sometimes ineffective is enough to justify to him inference that a being, that is to say a force, can now strengthen and now weaken, that a being's force can become inoperative, that the *bwanga* can "depart", "grow cold", or be "trampled under foot", as they put it.

So the criteriology of the Bantu rests upon external evidence, upon the authority and dominating life force of the ancestors. It rests at the same time upon the internal evidence of experience of nature and of living phenomena, observed from their point of view. No doubt, anyone can show the error of their reasoning ; but it must none the less be admitted that their notions are based on reason, that their criteriology and their wisdom belong to rational knowledge.

4. *The Bantu differentiate philosophy from the natural sciences.*

The transcendental and universal notions of being and of its force, of action, and of the relationships and reciprocal influences of beings make up Bantu philosophy. This domain is accessible to the ordinary intelligence of every normal "muntu".

If one desired to ridicule this philosophy or to give a childish caricature of it, objecting that its concepts do not rest upon the discipline of rigorous scientific experience, it would be as well to take care not to commit oneself to arguments more ridiculous than the pretended stupidity of these primitive peoples themselves.

Is our philosophy based upon scientific experiment ? Does it depend upon chemical analysis, on mechanics, or on anatomy ? Natural sciences can no more refute a system of philosophy than they can create one. Our elders used to possess a systematised philosophy which the most advanced modern sciences have not broken down. Moreover, our ancestors came by their knowledge of being at a time when their experimental scientific knowledge was very poor and defective, if not totally erroneous. The tool of empirical science is sense experience of visible realities, while philosophy goes off into intellectual contemplation of general realities concerning the invisible nature of beings. But no instrument exists for measuring the soul, though this fact does not exclude the possibility that experiences may occur in order to furnish intelligence with reasonable proof of the existence of the spiritual principle in life. It is the intellect that creates science. Indeed the experiments of the natural sciences, as also the generalizations of the philosopher ought to be made methodically and with discernment and analysed in accordance with sound logical reasoning. This presupposes always that one does not question the objective worth of intellectual knowledge. Happily, primitive peoples are no more tortured with doubt than our *subévolués* or the validity of human reasoning.

The subjective point of view of the Bantu founds the general principle and notion of being on the argument of authority and on their own observation of the constitution of the universe. That, I presume, is why this conception can be found among all the so-called non-civilized peoples. For the same reason it persists among educated natives and converts to Christianity.

The general conception of being which one may hold and the knowledge of the particular qualities of each individual being are two distinct things. It is not the duty of philosophy as such to include the defining of a particular being by describing its specific essence, energy, faculties, influences and properties. This belongs to the sphere of the natural sciences. And one can pose the question whether, within the natural sciences, unanimity has been achieved and the last word said upon the nature of the different natural forces which have so far been discovered.

Among the Bantu likewise, the same divergence of views and the same ignorance is to be found in regard to the imperfect knowledge of concrete objects with which they are in actual contact. They agree that many mysteries remain to be elucidated. Who but God can know everything, say our Bantu. God can give a name to each thing because he knows all beings. That is why the practical application of Bantu philosophy to the daily needs of life, to magical

6

practices, differs from tribe to tribe and from district to district. It also explains why, in comparing different territories, apparently contradictory proceedings can be observed, which none the less are but varied applications of the same general Bantu philosophical principles.

Beings, however, are known by their individual natures. So, as has already been observed above, the Bantu distinguish the external appearance of visible beings from the force and inner nature of beings themselves. But the inner, invisible force can concentrate or manifest itself more particularly in one part of the visible being. The vital force can be intensified and compacted and can exteriorise itself at what we may call a nodal point or vital centre. This vital centre, this nodal point, this particularised manifestation or sign of the vital force, is called "kijimba" by the Baluba. A wild beast may be pierced by ten arrows without dying, while another beast succumbs to the first shot. This is because the one arrow has touched the vital centre, or one of its vital centres.

Why is the crocodile so formidable a beast? Where is its murderous vital force centred if not in its ever-watchful eye that nothing escapes? And the symbol, the instrument endowed with the destructive vital force of Master Lion: where is it located? Obviously it must be in its ferocious tooth.

It is, then, very natural, from the Bantu point of view, that if anyone wishes to take for himself, or to make use of the vital force of an inferior being, he should try to procure for himself a like "kijimba"

which signifies and materialises the vital relation between the other being and himself [1]. It is, moreover,
the "kijimba" that one finds as the chief element, the
active principle, the source of energy in every "bwanga". Knowledge of certain specified forces and particularly of the corresponding "kijimba" is spread in a
relatively uniform manner among all Bantu. There
are certain "kijimba" of especially powerful beings
whose function is to add their force to the carrying
out of certain habitual activities such as hunting or
fishing. In these occupations one has expressly to
measure one's vital power against that of another
living being. There is a struggle of the vital forces of
the hunter and the prey. One must, therefore, be
strong in combat and arm oneself with all the forces
of attack, even those belonging to lower beings, in
order to assure oneself of power to destroy the prey.

There are certain general laws which enable one to
know and to discover the vital forces and influences
of certain beings. These are the "principles" which
some authors present as active principles, principles
of causality of the magic. In fact they are not the
active causes in "magic" or in the employment of
natural forces. They are simple signs which allow us
to discover and know these natural forces. So one has
read : "similia similibus curantur". Ethnologists ex-

---

1. The Du. adds : "Wordt elke levenshandeling bij de Bantu,
elk levensvertand niet met een signum bewezen en bekrachtigd?"
"Is not every transaction which is undertaken by Bantu, every
engagement they enter into, indicated and ratified by a visible
token?" (C.K.)

plain this by declaring that a force acts *by* likeness and *by* agreement. I have, I think, sufficiently explained that this likeness cannot be the causal foundation of vital influence. But the resemblance between the murderous force of the lion or of the crocodile and the intentions which actuate the hunter or the fisherman lead the Bantu to believe that the forces of these great carnivores can be used in the exercise of the trade of hunter or fisherman ; or rather, in the struggle in which they engage respectively against the prey and the fish.

Another law says that the living being exercises a vital influence on everything that is subordinated to him and on all that belongs to him. That is why every injury to anything depending upon a person will be regarded, as has already been said, as a diminution of the being of that person himself. "All property is rich in mysterious influences," said Burton in "L'âme luba". The fact that a thing has belonged to anyone, that it has been in strict relationship with a person, leads the Bantu to conclude that this thing shares the vital influence of its owner. It is what ethnologists like to call "contagious magic, sympathetic magic" ; but it is neither contact nor "sympathy" that are the active elements, but solely the vital force of the owner, which acts, as one knows, because it persists in the being of the thing possessed or used by him.

A third law allows the Bantu to recognize and discover vital forces or vital influences in certain cases. A living man's words or his gesture are considered, more than any other manifestation, to be the formal expression or sign of his vital influence. From that, if words or gestures lead to favourable or unfavourable effects as they are applied to a predetermined person, one may deduce therefrom that such a person exercises his vital influence, for good or ill, upon such other person. What one is in the habit of calling "magic of expressed wish", or "magic of mimicry", or "imitative magic", indicates this kind of handiwork ; but here, again, there are neither words nor mimicry that exercice a power, but only signs that externalise the action of the vital influence and make it known to third parties.

These three principles (maybe others will be discovered) fix the rules of research and of knowledge of concrete forces and of vital influences emanating from particular objects. They are in some kind the laws of the Bantu's knowledge of the natural sciences ; they are canons of judgment and in no way causes.

5. *The cleavage between the domains of certain knowledge and of uncertain science among the Bantu* [1].

From what has been said we can note the cleavage

---

1. The contrast between the two terms "certain knowledge" and "uncertain science" comes out more sharply, perhaps, in English than in French, but cf. Lalande, *op. cit.* p. 71 "approximatif". The Du. is simpler : "Wat staat vast en wat is wisselvallig en onzeker in de kennis bij de Bantu?" "What is absolute and what is uncertain in Bantu knowledge?" (C.K.)

between those principles and laws considered by the Bantu to be absolute and immutable and the domains of particular knowledge in which one feels one's way in relativity, uncertainty and speculation.

The general notions treated in Chapter II of this book are regarded by Bantu as absolute and invariable. Their philosophical and ontological conceptions, so far as they are applicable to being in itself have, for the Bantu, absolute and necessary validity, admitting of no exceptions. It would, therefore, be fundamentally erroneous to suggest that the conceptions and principles of the Bantu are essentially variable, uncertain and arbitrary. Exactly the reverse is true, at least if one is able to adopt correctly their subjective point of view. Their metaphysic, like ours, proclaims universal and unchangeable laws.

Even the general laws of natural science, of physics, and in particular the three canons of judgment regarding knowledge of force-beings and their influence, have for the Bantu a quality of general validity.

Nevertheless, when one comes down to the level of particular knowledge, the Bantu agree that one is in the realm of speculation and guessing, of skill and deftness.

And so, to know what particular vital influence has attacked a man to cause his sickness, one consults a specialist in the science of the interference of forces. In the same way, to know what "kijimba" will be able to restore such an one, it is not enough to rely on one's own knowledge, any more than to rely upon

the counsel of the first person whom one may meet.
In such cases, the wise thing to do is to consult a
diviner. Just as not everyone can read cards or be a
palmist, so not everyone can be a diviner. The exercise of this skill presupposes special knowledge or,
more precisely, the force to know.

6. *Is Bantu wisdom natural, super-normal or super-natural?*

We call natural such knowledge as man can acquire by the normal exercise of his faculties. Super-
normal knowledge exceeds the needs and capacities
of a human being, but not of a being created with a
higher order of intelligence. Super-natural knowledge
surpasses the capacity of every kind of created being.

From what has been said above, especially as to
the knowledge of the "force-being" among the Bantu,
it seems that their philosophy, like ours, makes no
claim to be more than the natural intellectual knowledge of beings. The general principles of the knowledge of forces and of influences also belongs to the
realm of natural, empirical knowledge of the Bantu.
Since the particular knowledge of the forces which
have determined a given event, or the knowledge of a
thing in its concrete nature and in its capacity for
acting in respect of certain predetermined persons are
only, for the Bantu, (it seems to me) natural knowledge deeper than usual; it is only in certain cases,

when the direct or indirect intervention of God or of some other superior being is postulated, than one can speak of super-normal knowledge.

These are deductions from the principles of Bantu philosophy as they have been propounded above. They are worth just as much as the hypothesis of their ontology itself is worth. I believe, however, that these considerations entitle us to reckon as worthless the omnibus expressions that hamper ethnological research when people are pleased to label established facts with such epithets as "mysterious" and with qualifications of "super-natural knowledge" or "indeterminate influences" and many like terms. In general, among the Bantu, we meet only with knowledge that can be routine or specialised, without ceasing on that account to be natural knowledge. In their view it is only in certains cases that one seems to be abble to run up against super-normal knowledge.

It seems convenient to insert here a parenthesis on what is generally called "initiation" in ethnological litterature. The "kilumbu" or "nganga", that is to say the man who possesses a clearer than usual vision of natural forces and their interaction, the man who has the power of selecting these forces and of directing them towards a determinist usage in particular cases, becomes what he is only because he has been "seized" by the living influence of a deceased ancestor or of a spirit [1], or even because he has been

---

1. Fr. "influence vitale d'un ancêtre prédécédé ou d'un esprit. . ." (C.K.)

"initiated" by another "kilumbu" or "nganga". The general principles of Bantu ontology carry the corollary that every man can be influenced by a wiser one. Anyone who is thus "seized" passes into a trance at the moment when the spirit or *vidye* possesses him, and it is at this moment that the neophyte acquires his superior force whereby to know and to direct forces. But in this phenomenon there is no question of initiation. Initiation occurs only when a candidate for "kilumbu" or "nganga" goes to find "a man with manga" and asks to be trained in his art. Should initiation, then, consist in what the master "nganga" tells his disciple (his child in *manga*, as the Baluba say) of the secrets of "sorcery and magic" ? The "nganga" can only teach his apprentice the different manipulations and ceremonies of his art, he can give him adequate training in the behaviour he ought to adopt in the higher life for which he is intended ; he can teach him the means to get himself into the desired state such that he can acquire force and knowledge, but, as I venture to think, it does not lie within his power to *give* force or knowledge. To possess the real knowledge and power of *manga*, there will not be, according to the view of the Bantu, any initiation in the English sense of the term. Only when the "master-nganga" has completed his work of educating the neophyte does the time arrive for his pupil to receive his power and his knowledge in the course of what has been wrongly called the "initiation ceremony". I presume that it is universal in the Bantu world that in the course of this ceremony the

initiate enters into a trance, loses consciousness and
becomes as if dead to his ordinary human life, to be
reborn from this catalepsy endowed with the superior
force and the exalted knowledge of "nganga" or
"kilumbu". It is indeed under the living influence of
his master that he is educated and reborn to this
higher living force, but the force and the power
which live in him come from a deceased ancestor or
from a spirit, under the influence of whom his master
equally acquired his power and his knowledge. Only
in this way can one explain the case of one or
another pupil who cannot be induced into trance or
rapture. His master is obliged to send him away,
saying to him "you are unsuitable". It is therefore
evident that a vital force must intervene superior to
that of the master of forces, and that it is wrong to
speak of "initiation".

These relationships, vital influences of the dead
upon the living, are daily bread to the Bantu. In a
greater or less degree these phenomena are familiar
to every *muntu* : they live in communion with their
dead and this living influence of the dead should not
be adjudged super-normal according to the canons of
our philosophy, but as a natural occurrence, as the
normal ordering of events in the world of forces of
Bantu philosophy. This is the point of view of the
Bantu which the ethnologist should adopt.

7. *Is there among the Bantu a knowledge which is not magical, that is to say, that is not knowledge of force ? Is their wisdom critical ?*

It has been claimed (Alliert : "Le non-civilisé et nous") that the African reasons half as we do (that is to say in accordance with a critical reasoning associated with the nature of things) and that he then abandons all reasoning and gives himself up to magic.

Thus it is indicated, for example, that Africans show themselves to be intelligent and reasonable in the weaving of their nets, the making of their traps and, more generally, in all their hunting crafts. They know what tools they should use to make efficient instruments, they employ an infaillible logic to contrive their ambushes. Then suddenly, as some authors claim, they give up all reasoning in order to depend for the success of their hunt on the help of the spirit of hunting or of the huntsman's *bwanga.* I think all the same that it is unsound to divide primitive man into two and to dub him inscrutable, illogical, or mysterious. It is possible that in gathering grasses, in retting them and in making baskets, fish-traps and other utensils out of them, the African sees no ontological agency at work. These are utilitarian crafts outside the sphere of wisdom or of vital force. Yet, one hears them say that these skills are given to them with their vital force. But they make a clear distinction between the aptitude to make a material object well and the power to devise instruments to

overcome and capture other living beings. The first is
mere child's play, the second a vital work. We need
not, then, be surprised to see the African go about his
professional aptitudes "magically", or to learn that he
thinks while doing so of the vital forces which he is
going to encounter. A man who is going to build a
canoe would never for a moment cease to keep in
mind his philosophy of forces. Any simple skill,
moreover, as well as the practice of magic, is shot
through and through with this dynamic conception of
beings. This conception, however, is quite a different
thing from magic, which is nothing but an evil practice equally prevalent amongst those who have a
more static conception of being and those whose
philosophy is dynamic. Coppersmiths and black-
smiths think that they will not be able to smelt the
ore, thereby changing the nature of the material
treated, unless they dutifully appeal to a higher force
which can dominate the vital force of the "earth"
which they claim thus to change into metal. As for
the huntsman, he is convinced that it is through a
higher vital force that he has the genius at his com-
mand whereby to construct his weapons efficiently;
and the dexterity to use them effectively in his combat with his captured prey. He thinks that it is his
vital influence, reinforced by the power of the tutelary spirit of huntsmen which has led the prey into
his gins. It would be difficult to find an activity or an
event of any importance in the lives of Africans
which is not associated with their philosophy of

forces by reason of their beliefs concerning vital influences.

The knowledge of Africans is not two-pronged [1]. They do not have a separate criteriology of the philosophy of forces, side by side with the reasoning of a national, critical philosophy. The philosophy of forces seems to them to inhere in their knowledge as a whole. They have no other conception of the world. Their philosophy directs all their activities and their inactivities. All consciously, their human behaviour is conditioned by their knowledge of being as force.

Can we say that our philosophy alone is a realist or critical knowledge, while theirs is not? If we understand by a critical philosophy, a philosophy founded upon observation of reality and upon deductions which can be drawn from human experience, I claim that Bantu philosophy is, from their point of view and for the ends indicated above, a critical philosophy as righty so called in our western systems. In their eyes, their philosophy rests upon internal and external evidence. If it were not so, it would be necessary to conclude that for lack of rational ends, their system would be the product of the merest fancy. But then the compact logic of their system would become an inexplicable miracle.

For the rest, it may be asked whether it is possible

---

1. Fr. "bifide" : lit. "cleft into two divisions". The context here will not stand the technical "dualistic". The English "bifid" (N.E.D.) is too unfamiliar, as also is "bifurcate". "Two-pronged" suggests the required basic union with separation. (C.K.)

to have a philosophy worthy of the name that is not the product of critical thinking. It is another matter to verify whether their observations have been made correctly ; or whether their deductions do not conceal errors of reasoning. A system of philosophy may be called "critical" even if it should be proved fallacious. If the term "critical philosophy" be reserved exclusively for an exact and true concept of being, one system only of philosophy can exist ; and it cannot be tolerated that differing systems of thought should have the word "philosophy" applied to them.

8. *Are the Bantu strangers to all experimental science ?*

That is a summary way of asking the question. We believe it to be justified because it brings it out in the false light in which it stands.

When we speak of experience [1], we think of something different from what the Bantu understand by "experience" [2]. In fcae of experience [3] we

---

1. The shading of meaning here is very subtle between "experience" and

2. "experiment". The Du. reads, "1) experientie... 2) experientie... 3)

3. Experimenteeren." The Fr. translation reads "expérience... expérience... l'expérience". His attention having been drawn, the individual reader must decide for himself in each case how to shade his concepts. (C.K.)

come to reasoned conclusions in accordance with our criteriology and ontology. The Bantu believe that they come to valid conclusions following theirs. We understand causality in terms of our static metaphysics, the Bantu in terms of their philosophy of forces.

Let us take an example to illustrate this. The Bantu know by experience which herbs and plants operate to purify the blood, to get rid of worms, or as specifics against infection. They argue, "This plant, this herb is such and such a force." This virtue acts no differently from all other forces, by vital influence. It can intensify or diminish... it acts only through the vital force of the strong, living man. Hence, therefore, the conditions, rites and incantations that are used when they have recourse to medicaments. It is not the first-comer, regardless of whom he may be, who will go to find a medicine. In order the better to assure the effective action of these forces, which are capable of being aroused, encouraged and directed, recourse is had to a person possessing special powers to this end. One seeks either the wisdom and skill of an "elder", or the skill of a "nganga". This awakening, this excitation of forces, is an everyday event among the Baluba ("kulangwila miji", "to stir up the roots"...) to the end that their virtues, their being, shall be active in aiding such and such a patient. In cases of failure, the inactivity of herbs which lack their curative power will be explained in terms of their principles of causal operation.

This confirms that among the Bantu all knowledge, even experimental knowledge, accords with their criteriology of forces and with their general laws concerning the growth and interdependence of forces.

CHAPTER IV

THE THEORY OF "MUNTU" OR BANTU PSYCHOLOGY

After having set out the Bantu conception of the world, their ontology and their criteriology, we must now examine their philosophical ideas on the subject of *man*. Only after doing so will it be possible for us to study their philosophy of human behaviour in their ethics and in their law.

INTRODUCTORY NOTE

The Bantu psychology which we are going to study is that which is to be found in the minds of Bantu themselves, not that which would result from the observation of Bantu by Europeans. It is necessary to see things from their point of view in order to understand the integration of this psychology into their general scheme of thought.

If we were to start from our psychological standpoint to study the Bantu, we should be almost fatally frustrated. Anyone who, for instance, were to try to

7

find the words which correspond in Bantu dialects with our notions of soul, mind, will, sentiment, etc. would be assuming that the Bantu divide men, as we do, into soul and body; and that they distinguish as we do the different faculties of the soul. This would not be a study of the psychology of the Bantu. On the contrary, it would deny the existence of any such psychology, in supposing that it can be satisfactory to translate our terminology. To prevent such a false start, we must, on the contrary, make a clean sweep of our own psychological concepts and prepare ourselves to finish with a conception of man very different from that which we now accept. The best thing that we can do is to listen and to analyse what the Bantu say on the subject of this being whom we are accustomed to call a "rational animal".

Maybe the results will seem scanty and the objection will be raised that no complete psychology emerges. Certainly, we should inter for good many of our nice distinctions, for many of the subdivisions by which we Europeans set such store have no equivalent in Bantu thought. It seems to me, however, that it will be worth the trouble of setting down together some vigorous basic thoughts out of what has been gleaned from the Bantu in this matter. Although briefly set out, this information can serve as a prolegomenon to later researches probing more deeply into the realm of Bantu philosophy.

A. *The "muntu", or the person.*

The notion of being, which the Bantu entertain with regard to all things, applying it to God as to created beings, has relevance and application also to human beings. This is apparent, moreover, in the language of the Bantu themselves.

Vital force, increase of force, vital influence are the three great notions which we shall find necessary at the base of Bantu psychology. It is on this plan that we wish to pursue this part of our study.

1. The "muntu" is a living force, a personal force.

The Bantu sees in man *the* living force ; the force *or* the being that possesses life that is true, full and lofty. Man is the supreme force, the most powerful among created beings. He dominates plants, animals and minerals. These lower beings exist, by Divine decree, only for the assistance of the higher created being, man.

It would be tempting to enquire in what the Bantu find this higher force to consist : to secure a more positive definition from them : to get to know in what principle they hold this vital greatness, this superiority to consist.

This question would correspond to one which we ask in the psychology familiar to us : in what exactly does the spiritual being of man consist, what exactly is this vital element that we call the soul ? But have we found an assured definition of spiritual being ?

Have we even as a starting point the necessary and sufficient conditions which constitute material being ? Composite, manifold, capable of sentient perception, bound to space-time categories : there are very many properties of material being, properties which are implicit in its very nature. Can one say, therefore, that these approximations give us a positive definition of the very nature of material being ? In defining mind or spirit we are no further advanced. Why and wherein is a being spiritual ? It must be in virtue of properties that we must try to define spirit. It is endowed with will and intelligence, it is not "aperceptible" by the senses. It transcends matter, acting independently of matter. These are so many negative or indirect qualifications which teach us very little in regard to the nature of being as such.

It would, then, be ungracious to reproach these primitive Bantu with being unable to supply us with a perfect definition of "muntu". On the analogy of our approximate definitions founded on our static notions of being, the Bantu will offer us descriptions of "muntu" in accord with their dynamic conceptions of being.

Man is the dominant force among all created visible forces. His force, his life, his fullness of being consist in his participation to a greater or less extent in the force of God. God, the Bantu would say, possesses (or, more exactly, He is) THE supreme, complete, perfect force. He is the Strong One, in and by Himself ; *I mwine bokomo bwandi*. He has his existential cause within himself. In relation to the

beings whom he has created, God is regarded by the
Bantu as the causative agent, the sustainer of these
resultant forces, as being the creation cause. Man is
one of these resultant living forces, created, maintained and developed by the vital, creative influence
of God. At his own level, man, by the divine Force,
is himself a living force. Man is not the first or
creative cause of life, but he sustains and adds to the
life of the forces which he finds below him within his
"ontological" hierarchy. And therefore man, in Bantu
thought, although in a more circumscribed sense than
God, is also a causal force of life. This definition
goes no further than to describe the relationships that
man can have with his environment, without therefore explaining ultimately his essential being. The
Bantu say again that the "muntu" has the power [1]
of knowing, "udi na Buninge bwa kuyuka" (Kiluba).
They regard knowledge and wisdom as living
forces [2]. We have already shown that true knowledge, true wisdom, consists in understanding the
nature and action of other forces, that is to say
metaphysical knowledge of forces, or of beings.

2. *The increase or diminution of "muntu"*.

This second topic is only an application of the
second aspect of the general theory of "force-being"
as held by the Bantu.

---

1. Fr. "force" (C.K.)
2. Fr. "des forces vitales" (C.K.).

What we wish to develop here has been more or less introduced already in the preceding chapters, especially in Section 3 of Chapter II which explained how the behaviour patterns of primitive peoples are centred in an outstanding value, vital force.

According to Bantu thought, it is, then, logical that the "muntu" should be able to grow ontologically, become greater, stronger ; and equally that he should be able, as "muntu", to diminish, lose his vital force and come to an end in the complete annihilation of his very essence, the paralysis of his vital force, which takes from him the power to be an active force, a vital cause. This state of the ultimate diminution of being is the fate of some of the dead. It is the condition into which those who have passed over fall if they have no means of renewal through those living on earth. They can no longer exercise their vital influence, either for the strengthening of life, or to the detriment of life by its diminution or destruction.

The living "muntu" is in a relation of being to being with God, with his clan brethren, with his family and with his descendants. He is in a similar ontological relationship with his patrimony, his land, with all that it contains or produces, with all that grows or lives on it. All acquisitions bring an increase of vital force in Bantu eyes : everything which breaks into this patrimony, causes it to deteriorate, or destroys it—that is to say, everything which brings injury to that which constitutes his vital force—constitutes a diminution of the "muntu" in himself, of the "muntu" in his very essence, which on that account will die, *kufwa,* in the sense that we made clear above.

It is always to accord with this conception of forces that the Baluba speak of "muntu mutupu" to indicate a man of middling importance devoid of real force ; while the "muntu mukulumpe" indicates the powerful man who has his part to take in the community. The word "muntu" inherently includes an idea of excellence or plenitude. And thus the Baluba will speak of "ke muntu po", "this is not a muntu", of a man who behaves unworthily. They will use the phrase of a newly-born who has been begotten outside the normal ontological, moral and juridical conditions of clan life.

There is the same thought in "mfumu" (chief) or "tata" (father), while they think of a man who has lost his force in calling "mufu" (dead) anyone whose human essence seems to them to be weakened by reason of his lack of power. When the Bantu thus indicate human categories, they do not envisage a classification based upon accidental differences, but rather a gradation in the essential quality of men in accordance with the intensity of their vital force. One of my colleagues struck the exact term for this when he remarked : "It is odd : these people do not speak as we do : they speak so "realistically". In fact, primitive language is very "realistic". Their words lead to the real nature of things. They speak "ontologically".

The quality of "mfumu" is added to the common humanity of an individual neither by external nomination, nor by singling him out. He becomes and is "mfumu" by endowment therewith : he is a new, higher vital force capable of strengthening and maintaining everything which falls ontologically within his cure. A man does not become chief of the clan and patriarch by natural succession through the deaths of other elders who had precedence and because he has become the oldest surviving member of the clan, but because primogeniture inherently supposes an inner secretion of vital power, raising the "muntu" of the elder to the rank of intermediary and channel of forces between the clan ancestors on the one hand and posterity with all its clan patrimony on the other hand. It never takes one long to observe the transformation on becoming chief of a man whom one has formerly known as an ordinary member of the community. The qualitative change is made evident by an awakening of his being, by an immanent inspiration or even, sometimes, by a kind of "possession". The "muntu", in fact, becomes aware of, and is informed by, his whole conception of the world around, through all his modes of knowledge, that he is now a true "muntu", endowed with a new power which did not belong to his former human status. He is no longer what he was. He has been changed in his very quality of being. Can one, then, be surprised that each accession of essential life is indicated by the gift of a new name ? Such is required to indicate that the "muntu" has been renewed and strengthened. In some countries, we are told, the initiate receives a new name at circumcision. Such seems logical enough

if circumcision is more than a mere surgical operation : in fact, a ritual (magical) act to strengthen
being. The carrying out of this rite is found, indeed,
according to Bantu ideas, to be in strict relationship
with the growth of procreative potency and to constitute its human vital power. The "mfumu" (chief) on
the occasion of his investiture, whereon his being or
his force is accorded increased status, receives a
name as chief. His former name may be no longer
uttered, lest by so doing his new vital force may be
harmed or desecreated.

3. *The "muntu" is an active causal agent who
exercises vital influence.*

Just as Bantu ontology is opposed to the European
concept of individuated things, existing in themselves,
isolated from others, so Bantu psychology cannot
conceive of man as an individual, as a force existing
by itself and apart from its ontological relationships
with other living beings and from its connection with
animals or inanimate forces around it.

The Bantu cannot be a lone being. It is not a good
enough synonym for that to say that he is a social
being. No ; he feels and knows himself to be a vital
force, at this very time to be in intimate and personal
relationship with other forces acting above him and
below him in the hierarchy of forces. He knows
himself to be a vital force, even now influencing
some forces and being influenced by others. The

human being, apart from the ontological hierarchy and the interaction of forces, has no existence in the conceptions of the Bantu.

We have dealt at sufficient length with the subject of the interaction of beings in the chapter on Bantu ontology, so that it is not necessary to review the particular relevance of it to their psychological conceptions. We have tried to formulate the laws regulating the interactions between beings, and have designated them causal laws. These interactions have hitherto been presented by ethnologists as magical only. Neither the whole thought nor the whole behaviour of the Bantu is magical.

In psychological discussions it is necessary always to stop to examine what we are going to mean by the term "the will".

The Bantu understand free will, the faculty which the "muntu" has of deciding by himself and of choosing between a greater and a lesser good, or between good and evil. They think that a man may have a "life-giving will ", or a "destroying will". A man's will may be determined in the same sense that in respect of life and the hierarchy of forces, he wills in accordance with that ordering of forces that has been willed by God. It is by acting in this way that the patriarch or the chief of the clan, the chief, the "nganga" (medicine man) is able to act as a lifegiver indeed, as a preserver and protector of vital force. A man can, however, be equally actuated by a will to destruction, a wicked will. His evil will (hatred, envy, jealousy) will have repercussions upon the vital force

of weaker beings through his mere willing a reduction
of their vital power. This wicked influence proceeding from the will to destruction of certain men is
known as "bufwisi". When acting with external
forces this will to destruction is known as "buloji", or
"kulowa" among the Baluba people.

B. *The name or the individual.*

The general notion of man, such as we have described, is a common possession of Bantu thought. It
is probably common to all primitive people.

Passing to knowledge of the concrete and individual being,   knowledge becomes more hesitant :
*"Munda mwa mukwenu kemwelwa kuboko, nansya
ulele nandi butanda bumo !"* (None may put his arm
into his neighbour's inside, not even when he shares
his bed). The neighbour's conscience remains inviol-
able, even for his closest friend.

What is the character of such a vital influence as
moves within my environment, with which I coexist ?
What is the intensity of its force, what is its action in
any given case, or on any given individual ? There
are so many things which cannot be felt with hands
nor seen with eyes. In this realm of action, witness
cannot be invoked in the European sense.

We have already indicated that the Bantu distinguish in man the man properly so-called ; and, in
addition, his different sense-evident manifestations :
the body, the breath, the shadow, etc. Direct know-

ledge of the living force, which is the man in himself,
is not given to everyone among the Bantu. It is the
privilege of the seers, who must be considered later
on.

1. *The general criteria defining the individual.*

The first criterion is the name.

The name expresses the individual character of the
being. The name is not a simple external courtesy, it
is the very reality of the individual.

An example will reveal the difference between the
acceptation of the name among Westerners and
among Bantu. If one hesitates as to the name of an
European and asks him, "You are called Louis are
you not ?" he will reply "Yes", or "No". If, however,
you ask a "muntu", "Are you called Ilunga ?" you
will elicit one of the answers "Tata" (Father) or
"Bwana" (Master) or "I", or "Myself, or "Here
I am", or "It is I" ; but he will not say "Eyo" or
"Ndio" (Yes).

Here is another example of this spontaneous way
of speaking. I had baptised an African baby ; and,
recording the fact in the register, I said to the
parents, "His native name is Ngoi then ?" Answer,
"That is he". "And his Christian name is Joseph ?"
Answer, "Yes". The native name indicates the fact
who the child is, while the Christian name is
something incidental, foreign, European. That is why
the parents could reply in the way Europeans speak.

"Is he called Joseph ? Yes, he is called Joseph". The first name indicates the individual specifically, the second name is an incidental epithet. The reply "Tata" or "Bwana", which may surprise the reader, will receive its full explanation later on. Here let it suffice to say that anyone who replies with his name to a reference to him does so in respect of his vital rank, the relationship of forces in which he stands with reference to the questioner who has addressed him.

The "muntu" may have several names. Among the Baluba there are generally three kinds of names. We distinguish first the *"Dijina dya munda"*, which is, so the Bantu say, the inner name, the life name, or the name of the being. This name is never lost. A second name is the one given on the occasion of an accession of force, such as the name at circumcision, the name of the chief, or the name received by a sorcerer on initiation, investiture, or on the occasion when a man becomes possessed by a spirit. Finally, there are names that one chooses oneself, or which one assigns to oneself, *dijina dya kwinika bitu,* a name which serves only to indicate the person, without having any profound relationship to the person or to his individuality. This last name may be changed or abandoned at the will of him to whom it belongs. Such are the *"majina a kizungu"*. European names as, for example, "Mashini, Petrol, Bececa, Motoka(r)" etc. Is it not fitting, indeed, that the "muntu wa bazunga" (the White's man) who is putting himself under the living, dominating influence of white people, should

have also an European name ? This furnishes us with
a novel example of the realism with which the African plays his life ; a play in which the philosophy of
forces is certainly no stranger.

Let us return, however, to the particular character
of the first name, the living unchangeable name, the
name establishing the individuality of the being. For
the Bantu, man never appears in fact as an isolated
individual, as an independent entity. Every man, every individual, forms a link in the chain of vital
forces, a living link, active and passive, joined from
above to the ascending line of his ancestry and sustaining below him the line of his descendants. It may
be said that among Bantu the individual is necessarily an individual within the clan. This relationship is
not regarded as simply juridical dependence, nor one
of parenthood. It should be understood in the sense
of real ontological dependence. In this order of ideas
we may say that the "interior name" is the indicator
of individuality within the clan.

Now, what is the clan ? It is the whole constituted
by the individuals who compose it. It is the ensemble
of interior names, started by the founders of the clan.
Every newly-born is therefore named with an interior
name chosen from the names, that is to say from the
individuals, who constitute the clan. The Bantu will
say to the newly-delivered mother : "You have born
our grandfather, our aunt, our uncle, etc." They will
say, "Such a spirit or such an one who has passed
over has been born to us." European observers generally believe that there is a belief in metempsychosis,

in the strict sense of the word. It is necessary to clear up this point, since the Bantu are quite unable to conceive an individual apart from this relationship, which has been improperly called metempsychosis.

Here are a few easily verifiable facts. The same ancestor can be "reborn", or can "return" in several living members of the same clan. You frequently come across several Ngoi or several Ilunga in the same clan, all called after the same ancestor Ngoi or Ilunga. It is already clear that if there is metempsychosis, it is not in the sense in which this belief is ordinarily held. It is difficult to see in fact how one dead Ngoi could multiply himself in several living Ngoi, each incarnating his *manes*. The Bantu will tell you that the little Ngoi is not identified with the dead. In fact, the birth of the little Ngoi in no wise puts an end to the existence of the deceased Ngoi in the world of the dead. The deceased Ngoi will become the "*ngudi*" (in Kiluba) or the "*mbozwa*" (in Kilemba) of the newly-born, who is his *majina* (homonym). This "*ngudi*" will be invoked on the child's behalf, and when the child attains the age of reason he will be taught to appeal on his own behalf to his "*ngudi*". Every "*ngudi*" remains the inseparable protector of his homonym.

So, then, when Bantu speak of the dead who return and are reborn, we must not regard them as speaking of metempsychosis in the classical sense that we give to this word.

How, then, are we to understand it? Is there a logically satisfactory explanation that justifies this

belief ? It seems that one can be found in reverting to
the theory of the philosophy of forces, the validity of
which will thus once again be demonstrated.

When a human being is conceived, the conception
is attributed exclusively and expressly among the
Bantu to the act of God. He is the creator, the causal
force of all life. When the fruit of conception develops in the womb of the mother and she begins to
feel the new life, the Bantu say that a human being is
already there. There is a being to be born. But they
ask who this being to be born is. The being is indeed
there, but he cannot yet be identified as an individual. If obstetric difficulties are feared, they will go to
the diviner, to ascertain who is causing delay. He will
sometimes explain that it is because an ancestor is
disputing with a spirit the right to be born in that
particular child. Sometimes he will reveal which of
the two has the better chance ; and in this way the
parents know whether it is Ilunga or Ngoi or
someone else who is coming into the world. Sometimes a pregnant woman is herself able to know the
individuality of the child whom she is bearing,
through a revelation made in her dreams. I asked a
Christian woman to tell me how the child which she
was presenting to me for baptism was Monga. She
replied, "While I was carrying I dreamed several
times that the deceased Monga was following me and
saying to me, "Unsele, Unsele", ("Bear me ! Bear
me !") and so I knew it was he who was following
me to be reborn in me".

The predeceased ancestor or spirit is not the cause

of conception, any more than it is his person which is reborn in the proper sense of the word. It is the human being who already possesses life in the womb of his mother (by divine influence) who finds himself under the vital, the ontological, influence of a predestined ancestor or of a spirit, or even of some deceased who, without really belonging to the clan, is found to be in strict vital relationship with the parents. Are not the ancestors, after God, dispensers of vital force ? And is it not through the intimate vital relationship of a deceased with his progenitors that the newly-born is able to be individualised within the bosom of the clan ?

Perhaps the idea can be better expressed by saying that it is not a predetermined human being belonging to the clan who is reborn, but that it is his individuality returning to take part in the life of the clan by means of the vital influences through which the deceased gives clan individualization to the newly-born, to the living fruit of the womb, that is to be born into the clan. This vital influence is preserved throughout the whole existence, since it is inherent in the very essence of the being.

2. *Another criterion of the individual, of the concrete vital force, is a man's visible appearance.*

Let us recall once more that in human beings the Bantu distinguish, besides the "muntu", or the being properly so-called, his body, his breath and his sha-

8

dow, etc. His vital force can express itself in a particular way in certain aspects or modes of external
appearance of the man, which we may call moments
or knots of high vital tension. The eye, speech, movement, symbolic acts, trances, inspiration, possession
are criteria from which the Bantu deduce the existence of certain vital and given forces, of vital influences operative in certain given circumstances.
These are the ancient and traditional proofs accepted
by Bantu of the existence of a concrete vital influence [1].

If one man curses another and the second falls sick
or meets with an accident, the malevolent word
shows unmistakably to the sick or injured victim that
the wicked influence that has broken into his life
emanates from the one who uttered the curse.

Let me repeat once more that it is not the eye, the
gesture, or, in the case mentioned, the word, that is the
agent of evil influence. And let us give up the use of
the outworn terms "symbolic magic", "magic of expressed desire", or "imitative magic". For the Bantu
there is the being that is force, capable of growth or
of diminution, a force that exercises a direct influence
on other forces. Herein is contained the very essence

---

1. Already the Baluba are following the example of European
judges and are beginning to speak of "witnesses" ("ba-temwa" =
"ba-témoin") who have seen or heard the matter at issue—all
that the European judge takes into consideration. Formerly
they stated the ontological cause, doing it though interpretation
of the criteria of the particular vital influence at work.

of the primitive concept of being. Besides this ontological concept there are contingent criteria perceptible to the senses, such as those mentioned above,
which allow the conclusion to be drawn of the existence and the presence of vital influences in concrete
cases.

CHAPTER V

BANTU ETHICS

A. *The norms of good and evil, or objective ethics.*

Man is not the ultimate judge of his deeds. He does not find the justification of his acts and omissions in himself. Transcending the free will of man is a higher force that knows, assesses and judges human acts.

Against the decisions and acts of the supreme human power, appeal can always be made to the transcendental power, from whom man has received his power of judgment, with the obligation to give account of his use of it.

When the elder, the patriarch, the customary chief has made a decision, the Bantu will say, as the Baluba have it, "I aye mwine" : "He wills it : he knows why he wills it : it is his business and his right." Nevertheless, whether they are absolutely sure that they are right, or whether they are convinced of the injustice of the human judgment, they will doubtless allow it to be carried out, but will claim the right of appeal before the Creator, Master of all human beings. Even while allowing himself to be led away, a man will call out : "Do what you will, you have the force to kill me ; but, all the same, I am God's "muntu". "Ne muntu wa Widye" (Kiluba). "He will judge us both : You have no right, powerful as you are, to pass arbitrary judgment on one who is not so much your man as God's man. It is not you who utter the law, your authority is delegated, mandatory."

Like all primitive (and semi-primitive) peoples, the Bantu turn to their philosophical concepts and no less towards their knowledge of God to draw out the principles and the norms of good and evil. They are not yet so civilized as to lend a new lease of life to our dead-alive rationalism of "lay morality". It seems, however, that it is the aim of some colonisers to open the way for their pupils to this "more civilized" system!

1. *Have the Bantu the idea of good and evil ?*

We often hear it said that Africans do not distinguish between good and evil, or at least that on these questions their ideas are those of savages, cutting morality as we understand it to ribbons.

It is true that many colonials take it for granted that Africans have but a vague idea of the Supreme Being, that they are convinced that no creature can come into his presence, that he always keeps his distance and does not associate himself with the daily lives of men. In spite of this prejudice, we thought it right to take the trouble to question Bantu upon this point. The influence of God in the daily life of man is recognized in many Bantu proverbs and sayings.

On the subject of theft, it is generally said that the African does not see the least wrong in it, that the only thing which matters is not to get caught. Lies and deceit, it is said, are, in African eyes, indications of subtilty of mind, countenanced by all moral assessment. They would not regard adultery as any infraction of morality and it would suffice if anyone caught in the act should agree to pay an indemnity.

Some, however, would concede that the Bantu are at pains to maintain the social order or peace within the clan ; declaring, however, that their care in these matters is devoid of moral content or of universally accepted ethical norms. Such authors are doubtless speaking under the influence of Western moral theory, according to which the social order is mere conformity with conventionalized behaviour. Such morality and moral law are evidently empty of fixed beliefs or unshakeable principles held from conviction. Ethnologically speaking, we have scarcely moved forward at all in presenting as Bantu ethics a bundle of moral precepts shot through with our own ethical concepts. We must get to know what the Bantu think. We must see whether the Bantu, from their point of view, go further than, or even contrary to, current practice in accepting transcendental norms of good and evil.

We can only admit it as an ethnological fact if the Bantu show us unchangeable and transcendental principles, in accordance with which they decide whether an act is good or evil, consonant or not with the vital order of things.

Let us emphasise that there is no need to regard misconduct as accepted conduct because it is often repeated. The orthodox ethical norm does not consist in the ordinary behaviour of men merely because they excuse their lapses by selfish excuses.

Moreover, I have heard Bantu say hundreds of times in various circumstances, "I bibi" ("It is bad"). What struck, and for a long time astonished me, was the note of profound conviction with which these two words were uttered, as if they felt, rather than knew, the distinction between good and evil. Thus it can be understood how they condemn in principle, and with all the force of their vital and indestructible wisdom, the destructive influence of the "muloji" ("sorcerer", in the sense of the man who casts lots). The Bantu likewise reject lies, deceit, theft and adultery, on the same fundamental grounds of the destructiveness inherent in them. They also condemn, as Bantu, various very widespread usages such as polygamy, child-marriage and other sexual abuses. In short, they know and accept Natural Law as it is formulated in the Ten Commandments.

Is it not disturbing to think that our authorities claim to be looking for grounds which would authorise measures against these abuses ! Yet we see these same authorities in the same breath taking repeated moral abuses for sacred customary law and sustaining the worst deviations from sound, ancient Bantu custom.

Every African before a magistrate repeats a formula very similar to that in use among the Baluba : "I am a man who speaks the truth, my words are in accordance with the facts as they were brought about and as they ensued, for I am a *muntu mukulumpe*, a worthy man." In other circumstances Africans will be heard to boast that they respect the rights of the person and of the goods of others. And is not the nostalgia of the old people symptomatic when they delight to say that "all the good old rules of life are being allowed to drift" ?

There can be no doubt that Africans have their ideas of good and bad. We shall show that their ethical principles are not, after all, merely left in the air.

2. *The roots of the knowledge of good and evil are bound up with their philosophy for the Bantu.*

The Bantu are still sufficiently primitive to be able to recognize the relationship that exists between the canons of law and the rules of morality on the one hand, and the principles of philosophy or ontological order on the other. In modern empirical science, the whole material world, all physics, all mechanics and the whole stellar universe are reduced to one single idea.

For primitive peoples the highest wisdom consists in recognizing a unity in the order of beings in the universe, from which they do not idiotically exclude *a priori* the spiritual world. Their whole ontology which can be systematised around the fundamental idea of "vital force" and the associated ideas of growth, influence and vital hierarchy, reveals the world as a plurality of co-ordinated forces. This world order is the essential condition of wholeness in human beings. The Bantu add that this order comes from God and that it must be reverenced.

Life belongs to God. It is he who summons it into being, strengthens and preserves it. His great and holy gift to men is the gift of life. Other creatures which, according to Bantu ideas, are lower or higher vital forces, exist in the divine plan only to maintain and cherish the vital gift made to man.

The strengthening of life, the preservation of and respect for life, are by the very nature of creation the business of the ancestors and elders, living and dead. Equally, inferior forces lie at the disposition of human beings for the strengthening, maintenance and protection of the life of the "muntu".

It is difficult to decide and to set out what may have been preserved among primitive peoples of what was originally revealed in explicit terms by God concerning moral law. But, the Bantu believe, the divine will finds expression in the world order, in the order of forces, which are accessible to natural intelligence. They infer this order of forces by their human wisdom and by their philosophical notions of the relationships and interactions between beings. Objective morality to the Bantu is ontological, immanent and intrinsic morality. Bantu moral standards depend essentially on things ontologically understood. Knowledge of a necessary natural order of forces forms part of the wisdom of primitive peoples. From that we may conclude that an act or usage will be characterized as *ontologically good* by Bantu and that it will therefore be accounted *ethically good;* and at length, by deduction, be assessed as *juridically just.* The Bantu have not yet, in fact, yielded to the subtilty which permits our jurists to devise a statute law divorced from philosophy, or from the nature of beings.

We have set out the norms of good ; conversely, the norms of evil run parallel to them. Every act, every detail of behaviour, every attitude and every human custom which militates against vital force or against the increase of the hierarchy of the *"muntu"* is bad. The destruction of life is a conspiracy against the Divine Plan ; and the *"muntu"* knows that such destruction is, above all else, ontological sacrilege : that it is for that reason immoral and therefore unjust.

3. *Human law accords among the Bantu with what is ontologically moral.*

In the same way as, for Bantu, it is the living *"muntu"* who, by divine will, is the norm of either ontological or natural law, so equally he is the norm of the customary law. We could show also, by an equally exact logic, that the "*muntu*" is the norm of language, grammar, geography, of all life and of all that life brings into relationship with the "*muntu*".

If the rights of property, land law, inheritance, ancient clan and inter-clan organisation or more modern political organisation—in short, of all legislation and equity—cannot be arrived at by logical deduction from ontological premises, it is none the less certain that primitive customary law, however intricate and conventional it may appear, falls perfectly in line with Bantu philosophy and ethics as we have described them.

All customary law that is worthy of the name (all that is law and not toleration of abuses) is inspired, animated and justified from the Bantu point of view by the philosophy of living forces, of growth, of influence and of the vital hierarchy. The validity and strength of the customary law of primitive peoples reside in its foundation in their philosophy.

On the one hand, *ethics*, that is to say the differentiation of human actions into good and bad in accordance with divine will or from the standpoint of the natural order which is but the expression of the divine will ; and, on the other hand, human law, that is to say the spoken differentiation of men's actions into good and bad in relation to their fellows, to the clan, or, more generally, in relation to human society, rest upon the same foundation of principles and form a single whole (cf. Possoz, "Eléments de Droit

Nègre", p. 30). Human society, in its clan or political
organisation, is in fact likewise ordered in accordance
with the principles of living forces, of their growth,
their interaction and their hierarchy. The social order
may be founded only on the ontological order, and a
political set-up which conflicted with this principle
could never be received as consonant with the Bantu
mind. It would be well to keep in mind the insur-
mountable difficulties aroused whenever an European
authority, actuated by the best intentions but failing
to understand the reality of Bantu ethics and Bantu
law, has attempted to impress a political set-up that
has violated the ontological order of the Bantu
hierarchy.

4. *The tenacity of the "muntu" in the defence of
   his rights is the consequence of his attachment
   to his fundamental wisdom and to his philosophy.*

The Bantu possess an ethical system proportion-
ate to what remains to them of their philosophy. The
knowledge of the higher laws is the clearer insofar as
they have been able to acquire and save a clearer and
more demonstrable notion of the world according
with their own ontology.

Confronted with the everlasting palavers of Africans, we tend to become bored to distraction and to
lose patience. But how can the African change this
approach to affairs ? The deeper his thought, the

more his arguments are rooted in his philosophical beliefs, in his wisdom and in his ontological behaviour, the more tenacious he will be and the more he will rise to defend his precious human rights. It is in defence of their rights that non-civilized peoples show their personalities to best advantage, because their rights, like their religion, are built upon the ultimate essence of their humanity, upon their conception of the world and upon their philosophy.

In African eyes, to renounce one's philosophy is to renounce ethics and law. His deepest obligations, founded on the unalterable principles of his philosophy and on his concept of humanity and plenitude of life, condition both the profound consciousness which he has of his rights and the sacred character that he attributes to them.

A person who confines himself to recognising in his juridical system simple civil, economic, or social obligations, can only claim, in law, simple civil, economic or social rights. The uncivilized man is very conscious of his rights as man ; and one is tempted to pay profound respect to the juridical conceptions of such a "savage" ; at least, so long as he himself has a practical respect for the rights of his neighbour on the same grounds as those which he claims for his own rights. This proud tenacity and consciousness of the Bantu in defending their human rights becomes, in the light of our better understanding of Bantu mentality, a human quality greatly to be appreciated. No longer should we see in it the uncouth short-sightedness of savages.

B. *Man good and bad : subjective ethics.*

Having examined the objective norms of good and evil, ontological, ethical and juridical, among Bantu, we should now study what, from the point of view of uncivilized people, the behaviour of the "*muntu*" ought to be, regarding him as an individual, as a member of the clan society, or as a citizen of a political set-up.

We must consider the Bantu notions of duty, conscience, guilt and responsibility. When and why does the "*muntu*" know and feel himself to be good or evil ? When and why does the clan or the political society pin the label good or wicked on one of its members ? What are the degrees of human goodness or human wickedness ? What, in the eyes of the Bantu community, are the aggravating or extenuating circumstances to be considered in relation to such assessment ?

1. *The pervert or destroyer ("buloji", "mfwisi", "ndoki").*

According, to the Bantu there is unforgivable wickedness in some people : total, superlative wickedness. In all branches of the Bantu family, the "*muntu*" testifies to an appalling terror, an intense repulsion, in respect of this diabolical form of evil. It is the "*buloji*" (Kiluba) which, for a Bantu, is as it were a perversion, the corruption of his being, a putrefaction from which emanates contagion to his relationships, a truly ontological contagion.

According to the Bantu, the most degraded crime, the most cynical prostitution of the sacred laws of nature, is the voluntary and conscious crime of destruction by the *"buloji"*, or by *sorcery*. Our ontological study has shown us already that it is not necessary to effect such destruction that there should be recourse to magical practices or manipulations, nor even to any external instrument. The perverted vital force by itself suffices to realise these destroying effects. This corrosive force can annihilate directly, by itself. The Baluba call this wilfully sacrilegious influence, which wreaks mischief against that sublime divine gift, life, by the name *"nsikani"*, perverted will. It is impossible for there to be any reason adequate to justify or to excuse such action of forces against nature.

All enmity, hatred, envy, jealousy, evil speaking, even false praise or lying eulogy, are severely condemned by the Bantu. To anyone who allows his envy or hatred to rise, the reproach is addressed "Do you want to kill me ? Have you *bufwisi* or *buloji* in your heart ?" Every premeditated act directed towards the destruction of the life of others is called *"nsikani"* ; and true *"nsikani"*, that which wickedly brings harm upon the vital force of another, is the synonym of *"bufwisi"* or of *"buloji"*. Such a *"buloji"* is held to be in the highest degree blameworth by the Bantu. It is reprehensible in the sight of God, the giver and preserver of all life. Since the *"buloji"* brings harm to the natural order, to natural law, and consequently to human law, the community has the right of defence against such an evil-doer, who spreads destruction and death, who brings about the annihilation of being.

2. *The evil will excited or provoked.*

The Bantu recognize lower forms of wickedness. They admit especially that a man may be provoked or incited by others to a point at which his good will in respect of life becomes a will to annihilate. A man may be caused to submit to such vexations at the hands of his neighbour that he is impelled in spite of himself to utter imprecations and to will the diminution of the vital force of another. In such cases, a man becomes blinded by transports of passion, his eye is no longer clear, the man so injured has black in front of his eyes. "*Mu meso mufita fututu* (darkness comes before my eyes)", the Baluba say. "*Bulobo bwamukwata* (excitement seized him)". "*Nakwatwa nsungu* (I am seized by anger)", they say again. Excitement, anger, darkening of the eye are not faults : these states of the soul do not constitute a moral evil and consequently they may not be classified juridically as criminal. These attitudes, these human feelings are not in themselves wicked vital influences, although they may lead thereto. Such states, the Bantu say, are in fact determined by external circumstances, things going awry, or misfortunes, evil will, or the injustice of other parties, etc.

Nevertheless, although it is admitted that man finds himself carried away into such states by circumstances foreign to him, it none the less holds that anger, even though involuntary, exercises a negative and wicked vital influence when it turns against other people. A man so excited no longer finds within himself a disposition of reverence towards life. He lives in an abnormal condition, in a state contrary to nature ; and this abnormal state, in conjunction with a will that despite itself has become destructive is enough to exercise a harmful influence upon those human beings who come into vital relationships with him ; and upon all the minor forms of life (of existence) against which his evilly excited will stands on edge.

Although their pernicious effects can be identical, there remains a fundamental difference between the wickedness of the sorcerer and the evil will of the man excited to evil. It would not be said of the sorcerer that his wickedness has *taken possession* of him, it would be said of him that he is wicked and that his will *is* totally bad. But of the man possessed it would be said that he was provoked by difficult circumstances and that he was *seized* by anger. So long as the man acts under the sway of anger, so long as darkness remains before his eyes, the deeds which he may commit will not be reckoned as faults against him. This must be quite understood as a gust of passing anger, since the choleric nature producing continual explosions, or a permanent condition, will be considered as an expression of the wickedness of the pervert, the destroyer. When the excited man recovers his calmness, when his anger leaves him and when he begins to give an account of what he may have said and done under the sway of his transport, he is obliged to correct his involuntary destructive influence in order to return to an attitude of respect for life and to strengthening it. As this anger caused by an external agent is, by its nature, thus exteriorised, he is similarly obliged publicly to recant his imprecations and maledictions and to give evidence of his goodwill, as soon as his eyes see clearly again. If, on the other hand, he is obstinate after he has become free from the transport of his anger, he is at fault. There is an evil will in him which may be imputed to him and which extenuating circumstances can no longer excuse.

It is useless to say that many Africans are still impressed by the anger of Whites. The people of a certain village, in spite of an order given by their Chief, had neglected to prepare a lodging in which I was to stay. My reaction was anger, recriminations and reproaches. The Chief, far from associating himself with my diatribes, begged me to withdraw my hasty and untimely words, "kokilo kosyana, Tata !" lest the village should suffer on account of them after my departure.

In another village in which I allowed myself to be carried away by anger the people said : "No, *he* is

not bad ; it is we who are". The only answer was to
acquiesce in what their Father had said.

During revolts, the insurgents and many others
have been in the habit of saying, "The Whites are
bad men, they will be our death." This was simple
truth, in that colonizers merely exploited them, systematically ignoring the human worth and the rightness
of the people. The idea, peculiarly Bantu, is under-
standable only in relation to their own conceptions.

The visible proof of the fact that one has dissociat-
ed oneself from all wilful pernicious influence is
given by spitting out saliva. This is done especially
when two friends are reconciled after a quarrel. It is
used likewise when those who have injured a third
party offer reparation ; after the so-called "*confessio
parturientis*" [1] ; or, again, after the farewells of a
father to his departing son if he has previously opposed his going. We shall have to return later on to
these particular applications of the custom.

3. *The unconscious evil vital influence.*

Those who have lived among Bantu have often
given striking illustrations of cases in which a man
finds himself accused of exercising a pernicious influence and is condemned by reason of the illness or

----

1. When a woman has difficulty in childbirth, the reason is
supposed to be that she is withholding the name of the real
father, which must be disclosed so that the child can be born to
him. (Note supplied by Mr. J.L. Pretorius. C.K.)

death of another, without his being convicted of fault, or even of any wicked intention. Often the elements of proof are entirely lacking and the miscarriage of justice is palpable to an European witness. And yet it is said that the accused, after making a feeble defence, submits to the declarations and decisions of diviners and ordeals, or to the sentence of elders and wise men ; and he accepts the penalties which are inflicted. Such facts are incomprehensible to the minds of European jurists. I believe that I have found an adequate explanation in Bantu philosophy.

The vital forces are under the governance of God, without human intervention. The hierarchy of forces is an ontological order, founded in the nature of being, not depending only on external agreements and on external meddling. All forces are in relationships of intimate interdependence : vital influence is possible from being to being without recourse to external intermediaries. The vital forces, moreover, are not quantitative, mathematical values ; nor are they static qualitative values definable by philosophy. They are active forces not distinct from the being itself, which function not only in themselves and on themselves, but forces whose actions can pulsate through the whole universe of forces, to whatever extent they are in vital relationships with them.

In a Baluba village, I happened to see a kid, all deformed. The people of the village said to me "The owner of that kid would be wiser to kill the creature, for it will bring misfortune on all the herds of the village". Many authors have noted that, formerly, Afri-

cans threw misbegotten infants into the river at birth.
It is well known that the Bantu carry their sick
outside the villages to care for them in the bush or in
the forest and bring them back only when they are
healed. I may be allowed to tell of an African in the
Stanleyville district who committed suicide because
he had lifted his hand against his mother. The reactions aroused in certain tribes by the birth of twins
are well known. Such an event, if not considered
abnormal, is at least extraordinary, requiring appropriate rites. In the Milambwe region, north of Kami-
na, two years ago, some hunters killed a five-legged
antelope. Nobody dared taste the game and it was
taken whole, as it was, to the Protestant Mission in
the district.

These examples show that Africans admit vital
influences that are absolutely unconscious. Every un-
usual phenomenon, every abnormal being is called by
the Baluba *"bya malwa"*, and these eccentricities
they hold to be disturbances in the natural order,
forces out of the ordinary, bizarre. Besides, if all
forces find themselves in relationships of influence
according to their vital rank, it is but a step to the
conclusion that a force, abnormal in itself, will usually if not necessarily have a disordering influence
upon the forces upon which it exercices its action. A
monstrosity does not constitute, any more than any
other being, an autonomous force ; but, like every
other force, it will have a vital influence and this
influence will be logically monstrous.

In some cases the Bantu seem to see a certain

automatism in the reciprocal influences of vital
forces, nearly as we see a necessary relationship between the cog wheels of a piece of machinery. It is
enough if one pinion is out of true to upset the
whole working.

The Bantu accept this unconscious influence, not
only between inanimate beings, plants, or animals,
but also from "*muntu*" to "*muntu*". They are convinced, as it seems to me, that the man animated with
the best of feelings, the best vital intentions, may
nevertheless exercise a pernicious influence. Who, in
fact, can boast that he knows the vital system to its
ultimate ramifications ? The general laws of causality
are known by every "*muntu*", in the same way as the
knowledge of the elementary laws of Bantu physics
belongs to the common patrimony. These especially
are the criteria whereby the vital forces can be dis-
cerned. Nevertheless, particular and concrete knowledge remains ever contingent. It belongs to the realm
of approximation and hypothesis. Seers alone have
the faculty of knowing particular things certainly and
yet... how often it happens that diviners are de-
ceived : "lubuko lutupile", as the Baluba say. The
soothsayer's error has miscarried, has "missed the
mark" as a hunter misses his prey. But a failure in
divination does not necessarily lead the African to
conclude that this means of knowledge is vain. In
their minds these errors seem entirely natural,
proceeding from the very nature of things and con-
forming to the nature and possibilities of our human
power to know beings.

From that the Bantu admit—and they are
thoroughly convinced—that man can by an act, an
attitude, or by his mere manner of being, of which he
remains entirely unconscious, bring harm upon the
ontological order of forces and consequently do harm
in this way to his neighbour[1]. I see no other
explanation, founded in Bantu philosophy, to explain
how Africans bow before an accusation when they
know very well, in their inmost conscience, that they
have not *consciously* willed any destructive influence
against life. It seems to me that they find themselves
in the position of the man who was learning to be a
chauffeur. He was convinced that he had followed his
theoretical teaching in every detail, that he had in no
way been guilty of an error in driving, and yet,
confronted with the cuts and bruises and the wrecked
car, he dares not deny that he had caused the accident.

Nobody, moreover, would deny that the Bantu
community recognizes the right to defend itself
against this kind of injury to its vital order. The "not-
life", the force destructive to life, cannot possess
rights, it is anti-ontological.

---

1. One thinks here involuntarily of the Jews, how they feel
"unclean" (Du. "onrein") for instance, as they walk over a
place in which anyone is buried. With them uncleanness and
ignorance go hand in hand. Christ confuted other false deductions of the Jews by the common philosophy of mankind held
by primitive peoples. ("Bantoe Filosofie", p. 81.)

4. *What, to the Bantu mind, are conscience, obligation, fault and responsibility?*

Bantu conscience : The moral conscience of Bantu, their consciousness of being good or bad, of acting rightly or wrongly, likewise conforms to their philosophical views, to their wisdom. The idea of an universal moral order, of the ordering of forces, of a vital hierarchy, is very clear to all Bantu. They are aware that, by divine decree, this order of forces, this mechanism of interaction among beings, ought to be respected. They know that the action of forces follows immanent laws, that these rules are not to be played with, that the influences of forces cannot be employed arbitrarily. They distinguish use from abuse. They have a notion of what we may call immanent justice, which they would translate to mean that to violate nature incurs her vengeance and that misfortune springs from her. They know that he who does not respect the laws of nature becomes "*wa malwa*", as the Baluba would express it ; that is to say, he is a man whose inmost being is pregnant with misfortune and whose vital power is vitiated as a result, while his influence on others is therefore equally injurious. This ethical conscience of theirs is at once philosophical, moral and juridical.

The notion of duty : The individual knows what his moral and legal obligations are and that they are to be honoured on pain of losing his vital force. He knows that to carry out his duty will enhance the quality of his being. As a member of the clan, the "*muntu*" knows that by living in accordance with his vital rank in the clan, he can and should contribute to the maintenance and increase of the clan by the normal exercise of his favourable vital influence. He knows his clan duties. He knows, too, his duties towards other clans. However hostile in practice inter-tribal relations may be, Bantu know and say that it is forbidden to kill an outsider without a reason. Outsiders, in fact, are equally God's people and their vital force has a right to be respected. The diminution and destruction of an outsider's life involves a disturbance of the ontological order and will be visited upon him who disturbs it.

The "*muntu's*" obligations increase in accordance with his vital rank [1]. The elder, the Chief, the King know very well that their doings do not involve their own personal vital force only. They and their subjects fully realise that their deeds will have repercussions upon the whole community subject to them. From that proceeds the scrupulous care that can be observed among all primitive peoples to protect the Chief, the strengthener of life, against every injury to his vital force, by means of a bundle of vetoes and prohibitions. These are designed to maintain intact his ontological power, his vital force, the source of the inviolability of all his subjects.

Fault and Responsibility : The obligations of the Bantu proceed from natural or vital necessities. Fault

---

1. Du. ". . . worden grooter naarmate hij hooger in levensrang staat."

or responsibility will, then, be proportional to the degree of evil will by which harm is done to vital force. Our account of subjective ethics has already shown the degrees of fault and responsibility as recognized by Bantu. They are :

1. Voluntary annihilation (*"buloji"* among the Baluba).

2. The evil will as externally stimulated.

3. Involuntary and unconscious pernicious influence.

Any further digression upon this question would be mere redundancy.

CHAPTER VI

RESTORATION OF LIFE [1]

Notions of penalty [2], compensation, punishment, forfeit and ontological purification.

We have followed Bantu thought in its science of beings (that is to say of forces) and their reciprocal relationships. We have seen how the Bantu understand the hierarchy of forces and their ordered or disturbed operation, their reciprocal powers of strengthening or weakening. Following that, we saw how man, the higher living force, exerts necessary, normal strengthening or abnormal disturbing, life-destroying influences on his environment. Finally, we saw in the *muntu* theory, how every "*muntu*" is constrained by God, by the natural order, by morality and by human law to exercise a normal benign vital influence upon its environment.

All this, however, only gives us an idealistic description of the order of the universe as it ought to

---

1. Du. "levensherstelling" : Recovery or re-establishment of life. (C.K.)
2. Fr. "sanction", Du. "sanctie". (C.K.)

present itself. The facts set aside this imaginary universal order, for the Bantu do not ignore the existence of evil, disorder, wickedness and *"buloji"*. Would they admit, however, that there is no struggle between vital forces, ideally known as life-givers, and the evil which they recognize in fact and whose real nature is destruction ? Could they conceive a world that is only bad, in which everything would be *"buloji"* ? Or, again, is there a real world, offering a workable order of things despite evil ? Vital force, order, law, are there so many Utopias, in contrast to which the Universe, the real world, is only evil, that is to say negation, illusion ?

Such is the eternal problem of evil which perhaps engages civilized Western thought as much as that of primitive people. Does right really exist ? In what form does God exist, how can he tolerate so much injustice, so many horrors as those which our times experience ?

Among Bantu the conviction is held that life is stronger than death, that law is greater than injustice, that the vital will is more powerful than the forces of destruction. For the final restoration of life, they found their hopes on the intervention of God. God possesses Right, the fulness of Right ; and he enjoys the sovereign use of it despite and against those who violate it. Even during earthly life he can be seen to intervene to remind men of the demands of his law by the infliction of injuries and misfortunes with which he may strike people. *"Kosepa memene, Vidye ukipanga"*, say the Baluba : "Do not deride a cripple,

God still creates defectives". Even in the ordering of
the hierarchy of beings he appointed a force for the
defence of his law within the natural order. The
elders, those who are still alive as well as those in the
world of the dead, have been endowed by God with a
formidable weapon : that of imprecation, malediction, or curse, or the withdrawal of the vital influence
of fatherhood.

Every man who has received vital force is endowed
with a right to life and is given means to claim and
eventually to revive his injured right. The vital force
given by the Creator is not a sham force, but a living
power capable of being strengthened, capable also of
offering resistance to the wicked wills which attempt
to destroy it.

In the same way the "antidotes" or "means" of
safety (*manga*) are potentially harmful and pernicious
for the owner who uses them heedlessly or irreverent-
ly ; and for anyone else who would make attempts on
(the vital force of) the owner or chief of those *manga*.

And so, not only are the Bantu convinced that there
is a suppositional order, ideally perfect but not rea-
lised, they also know that in the actual order, in spite
of the presence of evil, the real vital force possesses a
power of restoration of life, of restitution of right.
The vital force is, in practice, armed against the
destructive force : right and justice are strong against
injustice.

To grasp aright how the struggle between good and
evil is raised in the minds of Bantu, the struggle of

life against death, of justice against injustice, three
prior questions must be considered :

1. In what do evil and injustice consist ?

2. What evil and what injustice demand restitution ?

3. How are evil and injustice redressed ?

1. *In what, first and foremost, do evil and injustice consist ?*

It will be sufficiently clear from the foregoing what
the Bantu understand by evil : injustice towards God
and towards the natural order which is the expression
of His will.

Evil and injustice towards ancestors consist in
making an attempt against their vital rank. This occurs when a younger person makes a decision off his
own bat, or disposes of some piece of clan property
without recognizing the elders ; when someone goes
to a foreign judge to obtain his rights : or when he
makes a personal agreement with foreigners.

Towards a foreigner of equivalent status, injustice
has no longer the same character of "injustice" as
against the elders or brothers of the clan.

Nevertheless, just as in the sight of God, and as
before the natural hierarchy of forces and the vital
hierarchy of clan life, wrongs done to foreigners con-

stitute in their very nature an injury to vital force, a diminution of life. As such, these wrongs constitute an ontological wrong, an attempt against being, and therefore will be regarded as moral evils and injustice.

We have shown already that the life of the "*muntu*" is not limited to his own person, but that it extends to all that is fathered by his vital influence, to all ontologically subjected to him : posterity, land possessions, beasts and all other goods. In the same way as every good office, every help and assistance count before all else as a support, an increase of life to him who is the beneficiary, so every attempt, however insignificant, against the person of one who depends upon him, or simply upon his material possessions, will be considered as an injury to the integrity of his being, the intensity of his life. Every injustice is an attempt upon the life (so upon the vital force) of the person injured and the malice in it proceeds from the great respect due to human life, the supreme gift of God. In this sense, every injustice, every attempt against human life (against its vital power which fathers persons and things dependent upon it) is a stupendous evil, an evil measured in terms of the worth of life and infinitely exceeding in every case all calculations in economic terms of the loss suffered, but the measure of the outrage on life endured, which will serve as the basis of assessment of compensation or damages.

2. *What evil demands restitution?*

Since, in the minds of Bantu, the worst evil—and, indeed, the only real injustice—is the harm done to the vital force, it should be at least surprising that they should measure exactly the amount of restitution by the *lex talionis,* an eye for an eye. The exact restitution of an object stolen, or the drawing up of a tariff of damages, can in no wise be founded upon their conception of life as centred in man. How can they hope to measure good and evil done to man by criteria which are external to him ? From their point of view this overlooks the essential point : the re-establishment of the ontological order and of the vital forces that have been disturbed. Even when the restitution takes the form of a transfer of natural goods, it is considered as part of the re-establishment of life ; or, rather, as being a re-establishment of life.

We must study the customs of primitive peoples in accordance with their own norms of conduct, for it is only by thus arriving at universal principles from a comparison of established customs that we can isolate the laws of primitive peoples and systematise tribal law. If it is possible thus to separate the principles and the logic of a juridical system, one would still not grasp the rational grounds and spirit of a custom without having had access to primitive philosophy and the natural law as they conceive it. In his remarkable book, "Eléments du Droit nègre" (Elizabethville, 1943) M. E. Possoz revealed the great merit of recognizing that if the rôle of the jurist can be held to consist in systematizing a bundle of customary rules drawn from the practice of native law, it is only the philosophy of primitive peoples that gives us the rational ground and spirit of primitive law.

Now primitive law is essentially a law of persons rather than a code concerning good. It is law about the vital force and life, it is not a law of goods, property and their transference. It is only through the philosophy of vital forces that we can understand how reasonable, from the Bantu point of view, that conception of customary law is. Primitive law remains unalterably shut to our economic mental outlook, so long as we ignore its own grounds.

This theory can be illustrated by several examples.

When a Buluba agrees to lend 30 francs to a man of another clan, who is in a tight corner by reason of some extreme necessity, for example, to avoid distraint for non-payment of taxes, the borrower will admit, and all the Baluba will agree with him, that he has been "saved", "delivered", by the lender. It is not a question of lending and advancing ; or, to be exact, there is a loan in the Bantu sense (*kuluka,* as the Baluba say), that is, saving, freeing. Now it is a man who has been saved, freed. We see again and again that for his "liberation", which in our eyes is only the borrowing of a few francs, a man is ready to pay a costly glass-ware necklace, a rifle, or some other reimbursement worth ten times the sum advanced to him. If the case were taken before the judges, they would confirm the obligation, saying to the man "freed" : "Remember, here is your deliverer". I have often had to try to explain to this or that judge, and among them those of the utmost integrity and wisdom, that this was usury, swindling, and the exploitation of human misery. Their answer, always unperturbed, came from the depths of Bantu wisdom : "Has he not been saved ?" And they would finish their sentence with numerous examples, cases in which they themselves had paid sums equally out of proportion to the loan.

Very recently (February 1945) a village Chief, Kapundwe, confided to me a matter which had greatly mortified him. A friend in the neighbouring village of Busangu had entrusted a young ewe to him. One day, Kapundwe's dog was surprised while devouring the creature. Probably, Kapundwe said to me, it was not his dog that killed the ewe. Sheep abunded in the village and his dog had never taken any of them. Nobody could be found to testify that his dog had killed the ewe, but everybody had seen him eating the skin. Kapundwe began by giving an ewe to his friend, then another, then yet another, which made three ewes for one ; and he added moreover a sum of 100 francs. Naturally Kapundwe "disapproved", but what may astonish us in this story is not the demands excessive as we think them, but rather the fact that Kapundwe, while making a face about it, was yet disposed to pay such reparations without any legal decision or constraint. The Busangu man said "*Bisansa*" : "I am in pain, the loss of my ewe has hurt me : to assuage my grief at this loss, the sending of three sheep and a sum of 100 francs is not too much, for only then can I forget my grief and feel myself to be once more a happy man, a living man." It is likely that if Kapundwe had known certainly that it was his dog that had killed the ewe, he would not have dreamed of even complaining of his misfortune to me. The sheep lived with him, was under his vital influence. Therefore, everything which happened to the beast, whether good or evil, must be attributed to Kapundwe's conscious or unconscious influence.

Besides and beyond economic damages, the "*bisanso*", the sorrow, the wrong done to the man, constitutes the right to reparation. The man, wounded during his peaceful enjoyment of life, in the fulness of his vital force, the wholeness of his life, has a right to restoration of being. Material indemnities have no other significance than that of achieving the restoration of the man.

What, then, in view of this, is the function of judges? Is it to estimate and fix the amount of the indemnity which fairly recompenses the wrong suffered? It seems that according to former custom, the judges confined themselves to stating who was right and who was wrong, who was "white" and who "black", who was "strong" (in his own right) and who was "feeble" (and was succumbing). And one sees everywhere the zeal of litigants greatly exercising themselves to be pronounced white, to be able to put on "mpemba" (kaolin) or cinders, as material witness of the whiteness within, ontological purity, clear of evil vital influence, free from all destructive will. The party to blame is, on the contrary, pronounced "black", ontologically soiled, evil, because he bore harm to the "life" of another. In declaring who is white and who black, the judges have proclaimed the law. He who is acclaimed "white" and "strong" has the right to exact reparation for his life ; and the payment of economic indemnities, compensations, etc., follows then as a matter of course, although it may be admitted that, in an ordered society, authority sees to the execution of the sentences. However, the fixing of the amount of the compensation and the nature of the indemnity no longer appertains to jurisprudence, properly speaking. It is the injured man who, in theory, has the right to say what he considers necessary for the restoring of the fulness of his vital force. Very often the judges confirm and sustain the exigencies of the "strong" man.

It would be easy to multiply examples, but it may be enough to retain those that have been given with the particular purpose of making it clear that for the Bantu "juridical restitution" always has the sense of a "restoration of vital force".

3. *How evil and injustice are redressed.*

a) *Wrongs done towards superior vital forces.*

Faults committed against the higher vital forces, God, the ancestors, elders living or dead, are not to be considered as effecting diminution of the force of these beings. According to Bantu ideas, diminution of a superior force by a force subordinate to it is a metaphysical impossibility. Nevertheless, a lower vital force can ignore or hold in contempt a higher force, the younger may rebel against his elder. He who voluntarily acts thus behaves as if he wished to inflict harm upon a higher life, as if he were trying to weaken it, as if he were trying to usurp his place in the vital hierarchy. Such conduct holds in contempt the higher vital status of God, the ancestors, or fathers living or dead and amounts to a denial of their ascendancy. Although such behaviour [1] cannot harm the vital status of these higher forces, it does not consist solely in what we should call pride, irreverence, outrage. In the moral theory of the Bantu, it is a troubling of the ontological order, an attempt against the vital hierarchy.

Restitution for such a fault cannot be made in the sense of repair of the damage caused, compensation for diminution of vital force, but only by acknowledgment of the hierarchical order. This acknowledgment is made by means of propitiatory offerings, by ontological purification, by what has been called "magical" or "ritual" purification of the village and its inhabitants. The Baluba speak in this connection of "*koyija kibundi*", washing the village.

---

1. The Baluba call this behaviour "kibengo", a word usually translated as "pride". However, to say that anyone is of the same age, or of like vital rank as oneself, one would say, "we have *kibengo* towards each other". The true meaning, therefore, is "to treat as an equal" — quite obviously an irregular and insulting attitude in respect of a person of higher vital rank.

When an epidemic ravages a whole village, when fatal cases are multiplied, the Baluba no longer speak of "*lubuko*" (divination), nor of "*manga*" (magical cures), nor of "*kulowa*" (magical charms [1]). They conclude rather that the higher forces are disturbed : God, the ancestors, the dead ; in short, the whole higher order of beings has been provoked. Pagan Baluba are willing to pay dearly in such circumstances if the missionary will agree to "wash" the village with his potent "holy water" for they know very well why they are dying. Such misfortune can proceed from higher forces alone [2].

It will be well to state at this point the relationship in which the Bantu feel that they live with their elders and the forces of the invisible world (forefathers, ancestral founders of the tribe and God Himself) in order to justify their reaction in face of such calamities. It is necessary to define the juridical status of the living "*muntu*" in relation to the ascending hierarchy of forces going back even to God. It does not seem to me that the Bantu regard themselves as possessors of rights as against those eminent possessors of rights who are the higher forces. Their rela-

---

1. The Fr. reads "envoûtement", from "envoûter", which means to work injury by means of wax images : Low Latin "invultare" : see Littré. Du. "het noodlot werpen" : fate, destiny, to cast lots. (C.K.)

2. Footnote in the Du. Edn. "Wrong doing to superiors is thus really a disturbance and lessening of their life-force, and the restoration of that wrong must be a renewal of their life-force in its ontological purity and order." (C.K.)

tionship with the higher vital forces, the elder forces,
the worship which they claim to offer to God and to
their ancestors, have not, I think, the character of a
contractual pact. Let me explain. God is the giver of
life. Life is a free gift. The giver can be under no
obligation to the recipient. In contradistinction from
the Jews, conscious of a pact, an alliance between
Jehovah and Israel ; or from Christians who, relying
on Revelation, claim a new covenant, a new tes-
tament, between God and man, the Bantu are complete strangers to this idea of a contract either with
God or with the ancestors. On the contrary, many
Bantu proverbs recall that God distributes his bless-
ings and his woundings in accordance with his good
pleasure alone. They teach that the "*muntu*" has no
choice but to take what comes. They say that one
cannot hold a palaver against God. When Bantu are
asked if they do not sometimes upbraid their ancestors for not protecting them properly, they answer,
"How may we address reproaches to them, insult
them, or refuse to honour them ? Are they not the
great ones who already *were* when we were born ?"
The chiefs of the race, founders of the tribe, have
precedence over the living by so many living
grades [1], by so many generations, and they are seen
to be in consequence so near to God, that many
confuse them in practice with God himself, or very
nearly. Do they not constitute the supreme chain

---

1. Fr. "Précédent les vivants de tant de rangs vitaux" — grades
of vital force. (C.K.)

binding the clan to God ; and are not they the author-
ised mandatories in close relationship with all their
posterity. The supreme and immediate intermediary
of the superior vital influence is regarded by the
Baluba as the personification of that higher Force
and is freely referred to by his Name [1]. One might
suppose that children or descendants would have at
least a right to life as against their parents or ancestors ; that they would have a right to the support and
strengthening of their lives. Now, among the Bantu,
the very existence of children apart from their progenitors is inconceivable. They are unable to have
force except through their relationship with their
parents, for they have a right to it only in dependence
upon their elders. To say that ancestors or parents
have a duty of vital strengthening can be understood
only as an intrinsic duty, an ontological duty to
preserve the clan, a duty towards that force which is
superior to them or a vital necessity to their own
preservation. In his vital action on behalf of his
dependents, the ancestor or the elder is strengthening
himself, perpetuating himself in a line of numerous
descendants. It is consequently impossible for them
to will the destruction of the clan and in their efforts

---

1. Footnote to the Du. Edn. "It is not thought that the Bantu
identify their ancestors with God. Any official messenger from
the Chief would be treated as the Chief himself. He is, in the
absence of the Chief, as it were his image, the shining counten-
ance of his master; and what he speaks is none other than the
word of him who sent him. Thus Africans call me "Syakapanga"
(a name for God). Do I not stand as the representative of God?"
(p. 93).

to strengthen the clan they are necessarily "irre-proachable". They are, in a manner of speaking, "beatified". Only elders or patriarchs still living may be called upon for explanations, called to order and advised by the men of note and seniors, with a vital rank nearly equal to their own, each time that, by their behaviour, they jeopardize the vital force of the clan.

In any case, no child can enter into a contract with its father, so even less will anyone still living think of doing so with his ancestors. Such behaviour would amount to a repudiation of natural dependence. It would be tantamount to uttering his own death sentence. It would be in the nature of a revolt. It would constitute exclusion from the source of vital force which flows among Bantu by strict rules of primogeniture from fathers and ancestors. If mistakes have been committed against them, they can be made good only by contrition and propitiatory offerings, by formal recognition of the higher vital rank of his forbears and by his own ontological purification.

b) *Evil done to inferiors.*

The explanation given above on the subject of the vital relationships in the bosom of the clan shows us that an elder may do evil to a junior, to one of his descendants. He may restrict his paternal strengthening and so reduce his descendant to a diminished condition. He may abandon him while his vital force is thus reduced. He may even curse his descendants, or consign them to perdition. This diminution of vital force exposes *per se* those who are thus victimised to become the prey of pernicious vital influences. Although such an abandonment may not bear the character of dereliction of duty towards inferiors, as it would if they had autonomous rights, it constitutes, none the less, a fault against nature, an outrage against life. Such an action on the part of a father shows a disposition contrary to the Divine will, contrary to his own life's interests as being one who contains the life of all his descendants ; and hence contrary to the interests of the clan and its founders, of whose life-giving force he is the custodian.

Such a fault can be repaired only by a readjustment into right vital relationships with his descendants. Just as there is "malediction" ("*kufinga*" in Kilubu), so there is also a revocation thereof "*kufingulula*". If there are faults against matrimony (for example, extra-conjugal relations) which may have pernicious effects on the child to be born, this evil influence can be made good by the "confessio parturientis", or the avowal of the fault. If the opposition of the father to his son who wants to leave the village (to go to work for Whites, for example) earns him a malediction, there is also a "blessing", "*kupela mata*", to emit saliva, which can be done by giving the saliva to him on a leaf. This is the sign that the young man is not going to carry away the father's curse, nor his destroying will. If a man rebukes his wife for exercising a bad influence upon his children,

or as being the cause of their illness, he may invite
her to a *"kutompolo"* (to lament) so that her lamen-
tation may do away with her harmful influence, or
that she can supply proof that it does not exist in
her.

Reparation for the fault of diminishing vital influence for one's descendants consists always in re-
establishing a good fatherly influence. This restoration is always accompanied by outward ceremonies
which set forth and prove it.

c. *Faults committed in respect of equals.*

i. Reparation to the dead and to spirits.

Among Bantu, there is an essential and clearly
marked difference between ancestors and the num-
berless dead (especially those who have recently died)
who do not belong, properly speaking, to the ascending line of ancestors, by whom the vital influence of
the original progenitors descends to living posterity.

The founders of the clan, heads of the line, are so
near to the Creator that they are no longer called
among the Baluba *"bafu"* (dead), but *"ba-vidye"*
(enhanced, spiritualised beings). They are, after God,
the first strengtheners of life ; and they are, as it
were, for each clan the image, the personification of
God. The difference drawn by Baluba between *"ba-
tata"* or *"ba-nkambo"*, indicating intermediaries in
the ascending line of ancestors ; and *"ba-fu"*, ordi-

nary dead of the clan who were not Chiefs of the clan while living, nor are any nearer to being so after death, is, to say the least, characteristic.

With founders or ancestors there can be no question of a pact of any contractual relationship, as we have already said. They must not be injured or scorned, nor must they be threatened with a breaking off of relationships, for this would mean simply death for the living. When a disaster falls upon the clan, there must be no question of reproaching the ancestors, but simply of testifying from out of mourning to a re-established filial attachment to secure a new alignment with the vital influence of the forbears.

As we said above when we were considering Bantu ontology or relationships of being, and the right relationships that should exist between the ancestors or forefathers of the clan and the living members of the clan community, the living are in the position of newborn children in regard to their forefathers. This is considered entirely appropriate to right relationships. Indeed, their vital rank differs from that of the forefathers more than does that of infants from that of living older persons. Ancestors and forefathers still stand as the clan itself towards the living clan and towards each member of it as such. From them comes the vital force of the whole clan. Their veneration, the seeking of their counsel, sacrifices or gifts by elders of the clan to them, are the affairs of the whole clan community, though these functions are performed only through the intermediary of the living first-born of the head of the clan.

But towards *"bafu"*, ordinary deceased, all is different. Many dead of former days have been forgotten, have disappeared[1]. The dead of a nearer epoch, those who are still known, who were known as living beings, these are regarded as more or less equals. Between such deceased and the living, relationships are sometimes clan relationships, sometimes individual. Some relationships are urged by the natural order, or by the vital necessities of clan life, while others have a more contractual character. All these relationships, whether clan or individual, can be good or bad, rightly or wrongly ordained, just or unjust, whether from the point of view of the living, or from that of the dead. Restoration of life in case of clan relationship with ancestors will consist in renewed or acknowledged dependency on life. When the relationships with the dead are purely individual or contractual, restoration of life may sometimes consist in annulment of the past. Let us illustrate the point by means of examples.

A little time after the death of a *"muntu"*, account is taken as to whether the deceased is to be regarded as friendly or hostile. The diviner will decide whether an illness or a misfortune that has supervened in the interval following the demise of the deceased should be laid at his door. A deceased who has just brought injury to the life of members of the clan, or who, by exercising a pernicious influence on strangers, is compromising the clan which is responsible for his deed,

---

1. Du. "gone for good" (C.K.).

will be called among the Baluba "*mufu wa kizwa*", a
bad departed, a wanton, petulant deceased ("wa nsikani"). Those who are responsible for this deceased
will then hasten to make restitution for the wrongs or
neglects which may have been suffered in respect of
him during the period of mourning and in assuring
for him the honour which eventually he would have
due to him. If, however, the wrong has been made
good, or if the living do not feel that they have
anything with which to reproach themselves in respect of him, then it will be the deceased who will be
adjudged in the wrong if he does not agree to make an
end to his wicked influences. He has no right to
diminish, so as to enfeeble, the clan, either directly or
indirectly, without a proper reason. Such would be an
instance of "*buloji*" on the part of a deceased. Vital
restitution making good the evil wrought can only, in
such cases, consist in a struggle which the living
members of the clan will undertake against this pervert brother. This is the self-defence of life against
the principle of destruction. They insult and injure
such a deceased : an attempt will be made to drive
him away ; if necessary, recourse will be had to "*manga*", that is to say, to "natural forces" and, if that
is not enough, the ministrations of the "*manga*" man
will be sought, to get him to take away from the
deceased such force as may remain in him to paralyse his harmful actions, to prevent him from having
further dealings with the living ; and by preventing
his rebirth, which is the utmost diminution of vitality.
It is possible even to go so far as to disinter the

corpse, to burn it and to scatter the ashes. The Baluba say that he has been driven to the *"kalunga ka musono"*, or *"kalunga ka masika"*, which denotes the accursed region, hell, whence nobody has ever returned, and whence no influence is exercised. The deceased is then completely "dead", cut off from the living. And so ordered existence is restored in face of trouble, perversion, disorder. An ontological purification of the clan has taken place.

Another example : a deceased, a mere member of the clan, may follow a woman to be reborn in the fruit of her womb (*"kulonda"* in Kiluba) in order to re-establish his name in the clan. This constitutes a favourable clan influence, a strengthening which will not operate against or apart from the influence of the *"ba-tata"* (ancestors from whom the deceased himself received his name). Such an influence should not be denied—in fact it is always welcomed—and it would be wrong for the living not to give a child who is going to be born the name of one "returning". Such an omission would deprive the child of the strengthening patronage of the ancestor, exposing it to the risk of being born outside clan relationship.

But "come-backs" may *follow* a person for more personal ends. This may be so, especially, in regard to hunting. Such a form of "pursuit" will be revealed by some unexpected incident : an accident, illness, dream or omen. Such signs will not always be explained with certainty as warnings of such and such a spirit, or of one who has passed over, except through the intermediary of a diviner. The Baluba

take account of tutelary spirits of hunting ("*bakisi
ba luvula*"). These are spirits akin to the wind, which
have no material existence, have never been man,
bear no human names and are not born into the
human race. They follow the hunter to be honoured
by him, to receive offerings from him, to let him
enjoy the benefits of their protection, to secure
him good fortune in his hunting and to assure
him "force for his gun" [1]. It goes without saying
that the hunter will accept this precious help ;
he will need a place for prayer and for making
offerings to his "tutelary" spirit. He will call upon
this good genius as "my" spirit, or "my" ghost,
asking him "Help me !" But, nevertheless, should the
spirit or the dead come late with his help, we shall
see our worshipper exclaim, "What ! You pretend to
follow me while I am hunting and get my offerings !
I have done my part and you leave me in the lurch. I
shall do no more for you : never". And he leaves his
place of prayer, or destroys in his anger the votive
hut which he has built. Herein are clearly seen individual and reciprocal relationships, in which the carrying out of obligations by the one party is the
condition of duties being incumbent upon the other.
Injustice is here requited by reproaches and by the
ultimate annulment ot the pact.

Their original simple philosophy of the influence
and strengthening of beings has taken the road to

---

1. Fr. "un fusil fort", a gun with force to it. (C.K.)

more and more magical applications which have over-developed and smothered the simple clan community life and clan ancestor worship. We see now more and more individual practices, or practices of life-streng-thening, outside and apart from the clan hierarchy. In many Bantu tribes we are confronted with deviations contradicting the original concept of vital influence and of the strengthening of life. It is doubtless by objective study of this actual state of affairs that ethnologists have been led to conclude that the wor-ship of the dead was, among Bantu, in the nature of contractual, that is reciprocal, obligations. To my mind, it is more in accordance with reality to say that it is the end of a process of evolution, of metamor-phosis, that these contractual relationships with mut-ual obligations have set the ancient and natural law of the clan on one side. Many people, certainly, among the obstinate, conservative and philosophy-filled *Baluba ba Kasongo a Nyembo* still live in accordance with their philosophy and clan worship in spite of its abuses and magical excrescences.

ii. Re-establishment of life among living persons of equal status in law.

Among living peoples who are equals in law there can be ontological wrongs, influences that weaken life, legal injuries which can be made good.

The *"buloji"* or evil will cannot make good its destructive action. In the face of this evil, one remedy alone is possible, the liquidation of the intrinsic wick-

edness in the name of the rights of life. He who *is*
evil, who in his being *is* destructive force, must have
his malevolent action paralysed by every possible
means. This malefactor must be eliminated by being
put to death and, even, by incineration. The whole
community among whom the *"buloji"* lives can and
ought to take part in this ceremony. The *"buloji"* is,
in fact, Public Enemy Number One to all around
him. He no longer knows laws : neither ontological
law, human law, clan law, nor the law of peoples.

However, as we have already seen, there is also
wickedness which is excited, which does not pursue
evil as such, but which none the less issues in malevolent results. When one has business with a person
thus excited, one waits until he recovers his calmer
self, until his passion relaxes its grip on him. Only
then can one ask him to render account of the evil
that he has said or done, unless he has already given
his own explanation and has paid compensation in
those matters that require restoration. Such compensation, even if it should consist in damages for
material loss, has a deeper character : even a friendly
arrangement is always made with the express intention of serving as a vital restitution, or, if you prefer,
as a renewal in the ontological order. If maledictions
have been uttered (*"kufinga"*) they will yield to a
revocation (*"kufingulula"*) ; if an evil lot has been
cast (*"kulowa"*), the resultant evil influence ought to
be neutralized (*"kulobolola"*) ; if a misfortune has
been caused to an opposing party, the reconciliation
consists in the withdrawal of the misfortune (*"kusubu-*

la") and the restoration of the injured party to the full enjoyment of his force. Among the Baluba this is signified by touching the joints with an iron object, the symbol of force. Evil influences bringing results detrimental to communal hunting are neutralized by the confession of the party responsible ("*kutula mwi-fyaku*"). At each of these vital restitutions will appear the external proof of the expulsion of the evil will, the spitting of saliva ("*kupela mata*").

When a man who has caused a wrong through an evil will excited in him continues to feel resentment even after he has recovered his senses, he may be compelled to make restitution by force and by constraint, whether before a tribunal or independently of legal proceedings against him.

When wrongs have been caused between equals and within the clan, the Chief has domestic means at his disposal to persuade the trouble-maker, the disturber of clan life, to restore the vital order. He can reprimand, threaten, humiliate, place him after the injured brother in clan rank, or, worse still, take away his sonship from him, expel him from the clan and, in consequence, make him a man with no civil rights by breaking off his own fatherly relationship with this perverted clansman.

Finally, we have seen the involuntary wrongs which an evil but unconscious vital influence may cause. Just as the Jews could unwittingly and involuntarily become unclean (for example, by coming into contact with a tomb which they did not see), so the Bantu can disturb the ontological order without intending to do so[1]. Such wrongdoing must, however, be put right on pain of bringing down misfortune. Among the Bantu, restitution always consists in removing the evil and the cause of it from the community. The life of the community must be purified. It is thus that we must explain the custom of throwing into the river, the bog, or the bush creatures born deformed.

Every anomaly, defect and physical monstrosity and all illnesses are involved in some way with "*buloji*" and may have a maleficent influence by reason of the trouble which they cause in the normal order. Against all these evils there are purificatory practices, rites, prohibitions, ablutions, etc. Examples of protective measures of this kind abound among the Bantu of all districts.

4. *Conclusions.*

Although I have been obliged to confine myself to touching on the more outstanding characteristics, I trust that I have been able to reveal the Bantu view regarding the struggle between good and evil, right and injustice. It is a struggle which, for Bantu, can be ended only by vital restoration.

God expects recognition of his vital rank ; and he may exact it from men by inflicting injuries ("*bipu-*

---

1. Christ had to correct among his contemporaries many erroneous deductions made by primitive philosophy.

po") on their villages. Restoration in respect of the disturbing of vital order will finally be made in hell ("*kalunga ka musono*").

The founders of a clan and the ancestors employ the same means, but in a less degree, under the divine scheme of government and in conformity with divine decrees.

For men of humble station there is but one way to maintain and increase life, Right and the Good. The way is by the acknowledgement of higher living forces and by the maintenance of their own proper vital rank ; or, if they have deviated from it, then by their restoration in dependence on and attachment to the hierarchy of forces. Confronted with natural forces, there is by divine decree but one possible attitude : that of regular, reverent and wise use of them. Every abuse against nature in respect of these forces, every ontological sacrilege, demands restitution. Vital restoration, purification of being and sanctions as thus understood, are Bantu conceptions. Penalty, fine, damages belong to European legal notions, unless we modify their content to understand them in the significance of vital restoration.

CHAPTER VII

BANTU PHILOSOPHY AND OUR MISSION TO CIVILIZE

1. *The "non-civilized" and ourselves : amende honorable.*

If we are justified in the hope that we have plumbed the depths of the primitive soul in this treatment of Bantu philosophy, we shall be obliged to revise our fundamental ideas on the subject of "non-civilized" peoples : to correct our attitude in respect of them.

This "discovery" of Bantu philosophy is so disconcerting a revelation that we are tempted at first sight to believe that we are looking at a mirage. In fact, the universally accepted picture of primitive man [1], of the savage, of the proto-man living before the full blossoming of intelligence, vanishes beyond

---

1. "The very profound and suggestive analysis of P. Tempels restates most felicitously the fundamental bases of ethnology and seems to me also to throw must valuable light upon the spirit in which missionaries should approach the souls of 'primitive' people." (Jacques Maritain in the "Bulletin des Missions", No, 3, 1946, Loppem, Belgium).

hope of recovery before this testimony. On the contrary, as in the Biblical vision of the dead bones
which came to life, re-assembled and took shape as
man revived, we distinguish, vaguely at first but soon
more clearly and at length plainly, the true primitive
man whom we have misconceived. In the unnum-
bered crowd of the primitive masses, in the faces
falsely looked upon as bestial, we see the animal
expressions which we lent to these savages fade away.
It is as if, all at once, a light of intelligence illumines,
radiates from and glitters in these animal counten-
ances that have been thus humanly transformed. We
get the impression that these masses want to rise
from their alleged lowliness, clothing themselves in
the knowledge of their own lore and in their conception of the world ; and thus standing before and
looking down upon the small group of Westerners,
civilized indeed, but how puffed up with pride. We
feel that we should speak "from one school of wisdom to another", "from one ideal to another", "from
one conception of the world to another conception of
it". The gods are dethroned, the disinherited stand
before us as equals.

Ethnologists of the evolutionary school have already been perturbed by the "troublesome statements" of those who have revealed that it was
amongst the most primitive peoples, those least civilized, that the purest and most sublime idea of a
monotheistic God was to be found. Is not the discovery that there is such a thing as philosophy among
the Bantu going to lead to other "troublesome state-

ments" of the same kind ? It would seem, in fact, that the erroneous deviations from and inadequate applications of Bantu philosophy noted in the body of this book are generally of recent date. Older Bantu thought, healthier and more certain, can still be discovered in its most exact form among the most conservative tribes.

2. *A troublesome idea for us "educationists".*

The discovery of Bantu philosophy is a disturbing event for all those who are concerned with African education. We have had the idea that we stood before them like adults before the newly-born [1]. In our mission to educate and to civilize, we believed that we started with a *"tabula rasa"*, though we also believed that we had to clear the ground of some worthless notions, to lay foundations in a bare soil. We were quite sure that we should give short shrift to stupid customs, vain beliefs, as being quite ridiculous and devoid of all sound sense.

We thought that we had children, "great children", to educate ; and that seemed easy enough. Then all at once we discovered that we were concerned with a sample of humanity, adult, aware of its own brand of wisdom and moulded by its own philosophy of life.

---

1. Du. "Als het alles tegenover het niet".
   Fr. "Comme le tout devant le néant".
   "The Everything against the Nothing".

That is why we feel the soil slipping under our feet, that we are losing track of things and why we are asking ourselves "what to do now to lead our coloured people ?" For it is quite another problem to re-educate men fully formed—or misinformed, if you will—than to begin the education of infants, receptive to any and every impression. Even before we "rethought" Bantu philosophy, before grasping clearly its profound influence upon every act and deed of the "*muntu*", we were beginning to suspect, perhaps, that everywhere there was a Bantu way of thinking which deeply influenced their behaviour. We were even thinking that we must take account of it. Such a reality cannot be disguised, ruled out, denied or ignored by any conscientious educator. The question now is to know how and to what extent we must take this reality into consideration.

3. *The existence of a Bantu philosophy can reveal promising vistas to educationists.*

When as educationists we review the situation which this discovery presents to us, it is not generally to regret that we must abandon our former views with respect to the Bantu, since the new picture that is opened out to us is full of hope. If the Bantu have a definite philosophy, a profound corpus of wisdom and an established code of behaviour we can, perhaps, find in it a real foundation on which the Bantu peoples will be able to build their civilization. Perhaps we may say that hitherto we have been building on sand and we can grasp the several reasons why our educational work so far has failed to exercise as deep an influence as we wished. Possibly we shall feel regret for all the time and valiant endeavour that have been in vain, but we shall have the joy of cherishing the hope that we have at length discovered the true point of departure. We shall rejoice at having found "within" the Bantu something to render them more noble, without feeling ourselves obliged to kill first the man already existing. It is easy enough to deny or to misconceive the humanity of savages and, with the best intentions in the world, to destroy it. It will, no doubt, be more difficult (because it presupposes a strong leaven of humility, of generosity and of interest in others) to love the man as he is, to understand him, to put ourselves in his place, to acquire his mental outlook. And yet, unless we give proof of this humane love, how can we "educate" him, or gain his confidence ?

However difficult the problem may be, all men of goodwill must co-operate in it, to test what is valid in Bantu philosophy and what is false, in order that all that is of real value may be put to use at once in the education and civilization of these "primitive" peoples.

4. *What should be the educator's attitude towards philosophy in general ?*

It has been said that our civilizing mission alone

can justify our occupation of the lands of uncivilized peoples. All our writings, lectures and broadcasts repeat *ad nauseam* our wish to civilize the African peoples. No doubt there are people who delight to regard as the progress of civilization the amelioration of material conditions, increase in professional skill, improvements in housing, in hygiene and in scholastic instruction. These are, no doubt, useful and even necessary "values". But do they constitute "civilization" ? Is not civilization, above all else, progress in human personality ?

In his famous book, "Man the Unknown", Dr. Alexis Carrel points out that our mechanical, material, industrial and—more generally—economic progress has scarcely aided the progress of humanity at all ; that, on the contrary, it has contributed largely to make modern man less happy, by reason of the fact that it has misunderstood *man* and neglected him. On all sides one can hear today thoughtful people demanding that *man* should be recognized as the norm of economics and industry.

One of the best things which the Europeans have brought to Africans is their precept and example in the matter of activity. Industrialization, however, the introduction of an European economy, permanent raising of production—all that is not necessarily a measure of civilization. On the contrary, it may lead to the destruction of civilization, unless sufficient account is taken of man, of human personality.

Does not civilization consist, before all else, in ability to entertain an intelligent view of the world

and of life, to have convictions in regard to man's
ends, to be steeped in the enthusiasm of one's faith to
the extent of being ready to make sacrifices for it and
to suffer for it ?

What would a civilization be worth which lacked
wisdom and a live enthusiasm ? How can one pretend to think of a civilization devoid of a philosophy,
an ideal, and of inspiration ?

Finally, what education can be given without taking into account a philosophy and an ideal ; and
while mistaking the leanings and propensities of the
human soul ?

5. *What point of view should the coloniser adopt in face of Bantu philosophy ?*

If it is a crime against education to impose upon a
race of men a civilization devoid of philosophy, of
practical wisdom and of spiritual aspirations, it
would be a still graver offence to deprive peoples of
their own patrimony, which is their only possession
able to serve as the starting point of a higher civilization. It would be unspeakable for the white educator
to persist in killing in the African that human mind
of his which is the only reality that prevents us from
thinking of him as an inferior human being. It would
be high treason on the part of the coloniser to free
primitive races from what is of value, which constitutes a kernel of truth, in their traditional thought,

their philosophy of life, an integral part of the very
essence of their being. We have the heavy responsibility of examining, assessing and judging this philosophy and of not failing to discover that kernel of
truth which must needs be found in so complete and
universal a system, constituting the common possession of a host of primitive and semi-primitive peoples [1]. We must proceed with the Bantu towards its
sources to the point at which "the evolution of primitive peoples" was led into a false path by false
deductions ; and, taking this as our point of departure, help the Bantu to build their own Bantu civilization, a stable and noble one of their own.

We see more clearly every day that the European
civilization imparted to the Bantu is a mere superficial garb which has no deep impact upon their souls.
We see that those whom we have spoken of as
"*évolués*" have merely arrived at the point at which
they dare no longer profess their traditional wisdom
to white men : that they are thus, in fact, denying
their ancestors. Why do we not assist them to
perceive the true Bantu wisdom hidden within its
present errors ? Why do we not educate them to
discover and to venerate the ancient elements of truth
ever present in their traditions ? Why have we not
assisted forward their evolution from this wholesome
Bantu starting point ?

It must be recognized that the present results are,

---

1. Fr. "de primitifs ou de primitifs *évolués*." (C.K.)

in the main, lamentable. We see every day the count-less riches of the Bantu soul, but the general situation arouses agonised protests from us. We find ourselves surrounded by a horde of *évolués* who look upon their kindred with misgiving, but who are themselves at sea with life, to which they can no longer attach meaning. Our thought and aspirations were in fact presented to them in a totally unassimilable form ; and what we have tried to teach them of our Western civilization has remained something entirely foreign to them.

6. *Can we find in Bantu wisdom a healthy and stable base for a Bantu civilization ?*

The key principle of Bantu philosophy is that of vital force. The activating and final aim of all Bantu effort is only the intensification of vital force. To protect or to increase vital force, that is the motive and the profound meaning in all their practices. It is the ideal which animates the life of the "*muntu*", the only thing for which he is ready to suffer and to sacrifice himself.

This nostalgia of the Bantu soul for the strengthen-ing of life has been diverted. It does, of course, claim to put itself under divine direction and to limit itself to such natural forces as have been put within its disposition by God. Even the invocations used in magical practices are addressed to God in order that they can be made efficacious.

But, all the same, there is ceaseless deviation through the very frenzy of the search for vital strengthening, towards realities that are not life, or towards magical means of strengthening that are claimed to possess higher efficacy.

Man wishes to see the individual, to have proof of what he believes. He is led to substitute the symbol for the invisible reality ; and to invent mechanical and automatic means to force human life to move forwards. He puts himself in the place of forces which transcend him ; and even in the place of God himself. And so, whenever the accredited strengtheners of life seem to fail, he attempts the strengthening of life by his own powers. One after another he invents external means of safety and thinks of them more and more as agents operating on their own account, independently of man's own moral dispositions.

The Bantu proceed from the use of plants and roots to the "conditioned or ritual" use of forces, beyond the *kulangwila miji* (the reinforcing of roots) by a man who has become qualified or has been initiated, to end in *manga*, perceived, prepared and rendered operative by the one and only *nganga*. We see the existence side by side of these different remedies graded from empirical to magical practice.

The general principle of the interaction of forces is thus shaded and modified. The Baluba tell us that the greater number of *manga* or magical remedies are inventions of recent date.

Fortunately, this multiplication of external means,

intense despair has been spoken of as the chief reason and ultimate explanation of the slow but sure dying off of certain peoples in the Congo. But among those whom we have called *basenji*, "savages", the unspoiled people from the hinterland, the great majority fortunately still manifest a yearning to share our vital force.

What the great majority of the Bantu want from us, and what they will accept with profound joy and gratitude, is our wisdom, our means of increasing vital force. On the other hand, if we want to take anything to the Bantu and if we want them to accept the good things we have to offer, we must get to know how to give them in forms assimilable to Bantu thought. We must get to know how to present them as ways of increasing and strengthening their being, their vital force ; and not as means of annihilating the mind of the Bantu.

Our system of education, our civilizing power, should learn to adapt themselves to this idea of vital force and fulness of life. So that it can at once burst into flower and purify itself, we must devote ourselves to the service of the life which is already theirs. The view of the world, the ideal for life, the moral system that we wish to teach them, should be linked up with this supreme final cause, this absolute norm, this fundamental concept : vital force. If we do not go this way to work, there remains no other way but to extirpate completely the whole Bantu philosophy. Now, who could do that ? If we do not employ as our interpreter the forms of Bantu thought to propagate our truth, Bantu philosophy will fall back upon itself ; and the rift between African and White will suffer further cleavage, becoming ever wider and deeper.

There will remain with us a few renegades from Bantu thought whom we shall have decked out elegantly, housed comfortably, fed rationally, but without our having been able to prevent their becoming *évolués* with empty and unsatisfied souls—would-be Europeans—and as such, negations of civilized beings. We shall turn them into moral and intellectual tramps, capable only, despite themselves, of being elements of strife. When a colonial looks back upon the way that has been traversed, he will find it very difficult to assess the results that have been achieved. He finds it very difficult to grasp the psychology of those *évolués* with whom contact has been interrupted [1], or to know the real worth of these first-fruits of our attemps at civilizing.

However, it is the "savages" themselves, the "bush

---

1. Mgr. Pierad, Vic.Ap. de Beni (Belgian Congo) wrote to me in April, 1946 : "Your book is most timely in affording us an occasion for serious review of our attitude towards Africans. One after another of us must admit that we have more or less lost contact with them, that we are entering upon a period of emergency. . . Your book will greatly help all men of goodwill here in this colony —missionaries as well as laymen—to make a fresh approach to the native, grasping better the real facts of contact obtaining between him and ourselves. Only to the degree that we understand them can we attain to a love of them. Following the 'law of fear', which, it seems, exists at present in the colony, you present yourself as the herald of the new age of the law of love."

philosophers", who have made the point. It is they who have clearly seen it. Recently I have heard Bantu of the old school say, with reference to our modern product, the Europeanized *évolués* "These are men of *lupeto* (money)". They have explained to me that these Europeanized young men of ours know nothing but money, that it is the only thing possessing any value for them. They pretend to give up their Bantu philosophy, the living wisdom of the Bantu with its respect for life, for a philosophy of money. Money is their one and only ideal, their end and the supreme ultimate norm regulating their actions. They have no longer any respect for their old institutions, or for the usages and customs which, nevertheless, by their profound significance, form the basis of the practical application in Bantu life of natural law. The old philosophy, ancient institutions, ageless wisdom and the former usages of customary law none the less created and maintained the social order. Everything which was stable and of worth has been destroyed by this new value, this modern universal rule of conduct : *lupeto,* money. Such is the verdict uttered by these bush sages, so sadly misunderstood.

The proof has been given of the impotence of our economic civilization, our "philosophy of wealth" to civilize the Bantu, to produce *évolués* in the fine sense of the word. On the other hand, it has not been proved—the attempt has not been made—that the philosophy and wisdom of the Bantu are incapable of

serving as the foundations upon which to raise a
Bantu civilization. There are serious indications
which allow the conclusion that the attempt would be
worth trying [1].

7. *Has Christianity failed in its civilizing mission to the Bantu?*

Recently, in a still heavily populated district in the
colony, a learned conference took place of colonial
regional pundits... ecclesiastics being excluded. In the
course of this *conversazione,* the problem of the
evolution of the "Black Race" was discussed. The
conclusion of the meeting was recorded in a statement that several decades [2] of evangelistic work
was proving that Christianity had shown itself incapable of civilizing the Bantu. In short, the conference
announced the failure of the missionary work of

---

1. "To enter so deeply into the mind of the natives whom
one has taught as to be able to see things, not according to the
mental outlook of one's own race but following the paths which
they have trodden to reach truths which they have not yet grasped,
to see them through the eyes of their own minds, but from a
fresh angle; and to present them to ourselves marvellously
filled in, infinitely surpassing their own most secret aspirations..."
(*L'Ame Noire*, by Sister Constance Marie : Editions Grands
Lacs, Namur, Vol. II, p. 5.)

2. The Fr. "lustres" might suggest, ironically, Five-Year
Plans, but the Du. is "decennien" ! (C.K.).

Christianity. Let us allow that these gentlemen made
no attempt to propose any different or better way of
civilizing, beyond considering some suggestions such
as the amelioration of methods of cultivation, orga-
nised training for artisans, increased production and
intensification of trade... which monopolised the
agenda. There is no room for doubt, alas ! that in the
minds of these pundits it is in these categories alone
that *progress* and the true *civilization* of the Bantu
are to be found.

Let us admit, however, that it is not lay circles
alone that have declared that evangelistic efforts
among the Bantu have not been crowned with complete success. Certainly, some remarkable results
have been achieved : solid results which, perhaps,
would not strike the non-religious mind and which
do not allow themselves to be sized up in sensational
statistics. There are cases galore of generosity and of
dynamic effort which make us blush for ourselves.
Yet what missionary could say that he was fully
satisfied with the spiritual level of his Bantu flock ?
Something is lacking. There must be something
wrong somewhere.

Is this inadequacy inherent in Christianity itself ?
Or does it lie rather in the method of evangelization ?
Or should we lay the blame on the Bantu ? Are we to
conclude that the Bantu are incapable of attaining
civilization ?

For anyone who holds that view there can be but
one piece of advice : it is that he should systematically liquidate the Bantu ; or, more wisely, that he

should pack his bags and return to Europe ! Neither do we think that we have any space to give here to a discussion of the intrinsic worth of the Christian conception of life.

This book is addressed to colonials *of goodwill*. We see every day happy signs of the growing interest which the intellectual class in the colony is showing, in taking to heart its real mission to guide. I submit then to the loyal judgment of my readers from this class the reflections which I put forward.

The Bantu can be educated if we take as a starting point their imperishable aspiration towards the strengthening of life. If not, they will not be civilized. The masses will founder, in even greater numbers, in false applications of their philosophy ; that is to say, in degrading "magical" practices ; and meanwhile the others, the *évolués,* will make up a class of pseudo-Europeans, without principles, character, purpose, or sense.

It may be objected : let us admit that this aspiration towards the strengthening of life is to be found at the root of all Bantu tendencies. Where does that lead us ? What does it tie on to ? How can it serve as a foundation for a true civilization ? This thesis of vital power is only, when all is said and done, a product of Bantu imagination, a subjective idea which does not answer to any reality. We cannot give up our rational account, which is objective and scientific, of the real in order to pursue this path. Besides, if this idea has no reality, it cannot constitute an end, it cannot be held as a norm, it cannot lead to the real [1].

The weight of this objection from a purely rational point of view cannot be denied. Let us observe, however, that there is in our Western twentieth century a system of thought in which the strengthening of life is still received as a reality, that is, in Christian doctrine. That which for rationalistic Western science remains just a hypothesis, an unproved theory, to wit, the internal and intrinsic growth of being, in the way in which the Bantu teach it, is precisely what is taught by the Christian doctrine of Grace, founded on the assured rock of Revelation.

Even in our twentieth century, the Church has not ceased to teach and to avow this reality ; and masses of Christians keep constant the aspiration towards the strengthening of life, the raising of it, the taking of it into the supernatural, its participation in the constant intensification and internal growth of our life through union, living union, with God.

Catholic spirituality still teaches that God created

---

1. "It is quite clear, if Father P. Tempels is right, that the Bantu system of thought is not silly, childish or incoherent, though liable to corruption by magical practices and ought to be taken seriously." Prof. A.D. Ritchie, Prof. of Philosophy in the University of Edinburgh, in the "International Review of Missions", July, 1947. "This is not an isolated instance of this metaphysics. We find a taste of it both in Greek and in Christian philosophy and even in the latest developments of European thought. There is no need for astonishment and still less for talking in hushed, shocked voices at coming across well-known metaphysics." Rev. P.P. Charles, S.J., in the "Bulletin des Séances de l'Institut Royal Colonial Belge" 1946-2.

humanity by reason of the living richness of His own
Nature, by His Goodness, and in order to allow His
creatures to have a part in His Beatitude, in His
Love. This participation, we are taught, can occur in
various degrees and in ever-increasing degree. That is
to say, there exists on earth the possibility of vital,
intrinsic and supernatural internal growth. This intense spiritual doctrine, which animates and feeds the
souls who are in the bosom of the Catholic Church,
finds an arresting parallel in the ontological thought
of the Bantu. We arrive, therefore, at the unheard of
conclusion that Bantu paganism, the ancient wisdom
of the Bantu, reaches out from the depths of its
Bantu soul towards the very soul of Christian spirituality. It is in Christianity alone that the Bantu will
find relief for their secular yearning and a complete
satisfaction of their deepest aspirations. And this has
been admitted to me by I do not know how many
pagan Bantu. Christianity—and especially Christianity in its highest and most spiritual form—is the only
possible consummation of the Bantu ideal[1].

But it is essential to set out this perennial doctrine
in terms of Bantu thought and to present the Christian life that we offer them as a vital strengthening
and a vital uplifting.

If the Bantu cannot be raised by a Christian civilization, they will not be by any other. The superficial
Europeanization of the masses can only kill Bantu

---

1. Fr. "idéal", but Du. "heimwee" : home-sickness, nostalgia!
(C.K.)

culture. But just as Christianity could shape Western civilization, it has, in the truth of its teaching and in the human dynamic which it generates, the resources to achieve, to purify and to ennoble a real Bantu civilization.

8. *A last objection : the Bantu ideal will be a vital force exclusively earthly and materialistic.*

If the Bantu ideal were concerned with the temporal only, it would be difficult to see how it could serve as a basis for a higher civilization. Let us be objective. It is true that the everyday ideal for happiness is, with the Bantu as with us in Europe, tied up with the commonplace and the transitory. It would, however, be wrong to conclude that their aspirations are always materialistic ; and that care for higher things—moral, religious, humanitarian—is entirely foreign to them. There are abundant examples, some few of which have been cited in the course of this book, to prove that moral, legal, metaphysical and religious aspirations form a necessary part of all efforts towards a more vivid life. These few examples may suffice to secure that under the guise of paltry cares which fill so obviously the course of everyday life, there is to be found in the depths of the Bantu soul an aspiration, an irresistible allurement towards an infinite strengthening of life. All strengthening of life is to be found implicitly in this yearning, even

though today it is often so ignorant of its real consummation.

The Baluba say explicitly : You may have riches,
prosperity, a large number of descendants, and yet on
certain days be seized by a *"kulanga"* (yearning) or
"bulanda" (nostalgia) and find yourself *"kuboko pa
lubanga"* (literally, "the hand against the cheek" ;
that is, with one's head in one's hands) without
knowing why, beyond the fact that the human heart
is never satisfied."

That their ideal of *"bumi"* (life) is not limited
merely to physical force appears clearly from the
importance which they attach and the respect which
they show to the paternal or maternal "blessing" and
from the fear that they have of being "cursed" by
their parents. It appears again in their profound aversion from all that is evil and from all vital destruction ; and, in particular, from hatred, jealousy and
lying, whatever may be their backslidings in practice
in these matters. Their lofty conception of life appears, finally, in the spiritual idea that they have, in
their palavers, of social order, of right and of justice.
This expresses itself especially in the determination
which they manifest in the pursuit of restoration of
life, in accordance with the order of life willed by
God.

Instead of our being able to say that the Bantu
ideal remains materialistic even in its loftiest forms, it
seems to me that we ought to say, rather, that even in
their most material cares, the Bantu point of view is

dictated by a lofty wisdom in regard to life, linking on to their philosophical principles.

The least that one can say is that it is worth the trouble of verifying these theories in different tribes by a genuine trial. Such a trial has already been made by a number of missionaries and other colonials with astonishing effect in the spontaneous reactions of native listeners. It is, after all, they—Bantu of different tribes—who are the real testimony to the worth of the theory of vital forces which has been presented in this book.

ACHEVÉ   D'IMPRIMER   LE
30   AVRIL   1969   SUR   LES
PRESSES   DE   L'IMPRIMERIE
BUSSIÈRE, SAINT-AMAND (CHER)

— Nº d'édit. 64. — Nº d'imp. 269. —
Dépôt légal : 2ᵉ trimestre 1969.